150 RECIPES *series*

D0833804

CHICKEN *recipes*

CHRISTMAS *recipes*

CUPCAKE & MUFFIN *recipes*

FAST & SIMPLE *recipes*

GLUTEN-FREE *recipes*

GRANDMA'S *recipes*

HEALTHY *recipes*

INDIAN *recipes*

ONE-POT *recipes*

PASTA *recipes*

SLOW COOKER *recipes*

STIR-FRY *recipes*

STUDENT *recipes*

TAPAS *recipes*

VEGETARIAN *recipes*

150

GLUTEN-FREE
recipes

....

INSPIRED IDEAS FOR
EVERYDAY COOKING

CONTENTS

INTRODUCTION

Coeliac disease, which is an intolerance to gluten (a protein found in wheat, rye and barley), affects many people. Even the smallest amount of gluten can have adverse effects, so reliable gluten-free recipes are key for those following a strict gluten-free diet. For others (non-coeliacs), eliminating gluten and wheat from their diet may also help to resolve various ongoing health issues and improve overall wellbeing.

Although gluten is found in some everyday foods, a healthy, balanced gluten-free diet can still be varied and appetizing. It's essential to avoid all sources of gluten, some of which are easily identified (breads, biscuits, cakes, wheat pasta, etc), whilst other foods may not obviously contain gluten (couscous, soy sauce, lager, malted milk drinks, etc). If you are

unsure about a food, then it's best to avoid it, but food packaging should highlight any potential allergens, including gluten. Oats don't contain gluten, but they do contain a protein similar to gluten, which may cause an adverse reaction in those with severe coeliac disease or gluten-intolerance.

A gluten-free diet need not be mundane or unappealing and can be full of flavour. Many foods are naturally gluten-free, plus a good range of manufactured gluten-free foods and ingredients is readily available. Preparing tasty gluten-free dishes at home is easily achievable, but do ensure that gluten-free ingredients, plus any equipment used for preparing and cooking meals, are kept separate to avoid any cross-contamination.

This comprehensive collection of delicious and nutritious gluten-free recipes is the perfect way forward, and will inspire you to prepare and cook appetizing gluten-free recipes to suit all occasions and appetites.

The first chapter features an amazing selection of breakfasts and juices, providing a great way to start your day. You'll also find breakfast-in-a-bowl options like Quinoa Porridge or Berry Crunch, plus easy egg-baked dishes such as Plum Pancakes, Sausage & Egg Sizzle or Potato & Onion Frittata.

If you prefer breakfast on the run, Blueberry Bars or one of the super smoothies or shakes will energize you as you start your day.

Next up we focus on a selection of scrumptious snacks and light bites, from tantalizing tacos and tzatziki to ever-popular popcorn, pakoras, focaccia and flatbreads. Top picks include Prawn & Mango Skewers, Roast Kale Crisps and Spicy Falafels.

An appetizing assortment of tasty lunches features soups, salads, fritters, pizzas and pilafs. Keep chills at bay with soul-warming soups such as Spicy Tomato, Tamarind & Ginger Soup, or opt for a nourishing lunch bowl such as a Sweet Roots Bowl. Lighter lunch options include Lemon Chicken Courgetti and Scallops with Pea Purée, or for flavour-packed lunches featuring quinoa, a popular gluten-free grain, choose from Black Bean & Quinoa Burritos or Quinoa & Walnut Tabbouleh.

Turn to the next chapter for some fantastic family main meals. Meat, fish or vegetable-based mains all take centre stage, from pleasing pies and pasta to superb stews, stir-fries and steaks. Meaty mouthfuls include White Chicken Chilli, Lamb Koftas and Chimichurri Steak, whereas dishes such as Coconut Fish Curry and Grilled Sea Bass with Fried Quinoa are perfect for fish lovers. If you prefer a vegetarian main course, be tempted by delights such as Pumpkin & Chestnut Risotto or Squash & Red Pepper Pie.

To satisfy sweet cravings, there's something for everyone in our final chapter of brilliant bakes and decadent desserts, all of which are perfect for sharing. We concentrate on fabulous homemade cakes and bakes, many made with alternative (gluten-free) flours, including cookies, bites and bars, as well as some choice desserts such as puddings, pies and fruit kebabs. For enticing sweet treats, try temptations such as fuss-free Cookies & Cream Cupcakes or Apricot & Coconut Bars, or for delicious hot or cold desserts, pick family favourites such as Pecan Pie or Plum and Hazelnut Crumble, or mouthwatering Mango Cheesecake.

INTRODUCTION

BREAKFASTS & JUICES

QUINOA PORRIDGE WITH CARAMELIZED BANANA

Serves: 2　　　　**Prep: 5 mins**　　　　**Cook: 25 mins**

Ingredients

1 x 400 ml/14 fl oz can coconut milk

¼ tsp ground nutmeg

½ vanilla pod, split

100 g/3½ oz quinoa

1½ tbsp light honey

1 large banana

25 g/1 oz unsalted butter

25 g/1 oz soft brown sugar

pinch of salt

25 g/1 oz coconut flakes, toasted

1 tbsp sesame seeds, toasted

Method

1 Pour 300 ml/10 fl oz coconut milk into a medium-sized pan over a low heat. Add the nutmeg and vanilla pod and bring to a simmer. Add the quinoa, bring to the boil and cook for 10–15 minutes.

2 Lower the heat, stir through the honey and simmer for a further 5 minutes. Remove from the heat and take out the vanilla pod. Stir through the remaining milk and leave covered while you halve the banana lengthways, then halve again.

3 Place a medium-sized frying pan over a medium–high heat and melt the butter and brown sugar with the salt until the mixture starts to foam. Add the sliced banana and fry it gently on both sides for 3–4 minutes, or until the banana starts to brown and become caramelized.

4 Spoon the porridge into two bowls and top with the banana, toasted coconut flakes and sesame seeds. Serve immediately.

RAW CARROT, APPLE & GOJI BIRCHER MUESLI

Serves: 4   **Prep: 15 mins**   **Cook: none**

Ingredients

125 g/4½ oz
buckwheat flakes

1 carrot, grated

2 red-skinned apples

150 ml/5 fl oz apple juice

150 ml/5 fl oz almond milk

1½ tbsp dried goji berries

2 tbsp chopped hazelnuts

2 tbsp chopped
dried apricots

1½ tbsp shelled
pistachio nuts

1 tbsp sunflower seeds

Method

1 Put the buckwheat flakes and carrot in a
large bowl. Core, thinly slice and chop one of
the apples and add to the bowl. Stir the bowl
contents well until thoroughly combined. Stir
in the apple juice, almond milk and 1 tablespoon
of the goji berries. Cover and leave overnight in
the refrigerator.

2 Stir the hazelnuts into the bowl. Core, thinly slice
and chop the remaining apple.

3 Divide the muesli between serving dishes
and sprinkle the apple, remaining goji berries,
apricots, pistachio nuts and sunflower seeds
over the muesli. Serve immediately.

COCONUT POWER BOWL

Serves: 4   **Prep: 20 mins**   **Cook: 15 mins**

Ingredients

100 g/3½ oz coconut oil

1 tbsp honey

2 tbsp dark muscovado sugar

100 g/3½ oz quinoa flakes

150 g/5½ oz gluten-free rolled oats

3 tbsp desiccated coconut

½ tsp ground cinnamon

1 tbsp dried cranberries

1 tbsp chopped pecan nuts

2 bananas, peeled and chopped

55 g/2 oz walnuts

200 ml/7 fl oz coconut milk

1 tsp ground cinnamon

100 g/3½ oz raspberries

15 g/½ oz fresh mint leaves

2 tbsp maple syrup

Method

1 Preheat the oven to 180°C/350°F/Gas Mark 4. Put the coconut oil, honey and sugar into a saucepan over a low heat and heat, stirring, until the sugar has dissolved.

2 Remove from the heat and stir in the quinoa flakes, 55 g/2 oz of the oats, 2 tablespoons of the desiccated coconut, the cinnamon, cranberries and pecan nuts. Mix well to combine.

3 Spread the mixture over a baking sheet and bake in the preheated oven for 15 minutes, stirring halfway through the cooking time.

4 Remove from the oven, spoon into a bowl and leave to cool.

5 Meanwhile, place the bananas, the remaining oats, the walnuts and coconut milk in a food processor and process until almost smooth.

6 Pour into four bowls and add the granola. Top with the cinnamon, raspberries, mint, the remaining desiccated coconut, and a drizzle of maple syrup.

BERRY CRUNCH

Serves: 4

Prep: 15 mins
plus standing

Cook: 5 mins

Ingredients

75 g/2¾ oz rice, buckwheat or millet flakes, or a mixture

4 tbsp clear honey

500 g/1 lb 2 oz thick natural yogurt

finely grated rind of 1 orange

225 g/8 oz frozen mixed berries, partially thawed, plus extra to decorate

Method

1 Heat a dry frying pan over a medium heat, add the flakes and toast, shaking the pan, for 1 minute. Add half the honey and stir to coat the flakes. Cook, stirring constantly, until the flakes turn golden brown and slightly crisp.

2 Put the yogurt into a bowl and stir in the remaining honey and the orange rind. Gently stir in the berries, reserving a few to decorate. Leave for 10–15 minutes for the berries to release their juices, then stir again to give a swirl of colour.

3 To serve, spoon a layer of flakes into the bottom of four glasses, then top with a layer of the berry yogurt. Sprinkle with another layer of flakes and add another layer of the yogurt. Decorate with the reserved berries.

MAPLE BAKED OATS WITH PLUMS

Serves: 6   **Prep: 10 mins**   **Cook: 35–40 mins**

Ingredients

500 ml/17 fl oz semi-skimmed milk

2 eggs

35 g/1¼ oz unsalted butter, melted, plus 10 g/¼ oz, for greasing

60 g/2¼ oz dark brown sugar

75 ml/2½ fl oz maple syrup

4 ripe plums, stoned and cut into 8 pieces

1 large cooking apple, peeled and cut into 1 cm/½ inch cubes

200 g/7 oz gluten-free rolled oats

1 tsp gluten-free baking powder

1 tsp cinnamon

pinch of salt

50 g/1¾ oz flaked almonds

Method

1 Preheat the oven to 180°C/350°F/Gas Mark 4.

2 In a small bowl or jug, gently whisk the milk, eggs, melted butter, 2 tablespoons of the sugar and the maple syrup.

3 Grease the bottom of a 2 litre/3½ pint ovenproof dish and put in half of the plums, the apple cubes, oats, baking powder, cinnamon and salt. Mix everything together using your hands or a large spoon.

4 Gently pour the milk mixture over the fruit mixture and let everything soak for a few minutes.

5 Sprinkle over the remaining plums, the almonds and the remaining sugar.

6 Bake for 35–40 minutes, until the milk has been fully absorbed. Serve warm.

APPLE &
SEED MUESLI

Serves: 10   **Prep: 15 mins**   **Cook: 5 mins**

Ingredients

75 g/2¾ oz sunflower seeds

50 g/1¾ oz pumpkin seeds

90 g/3¼ oz shelled
hazelnuts, roughly chopped

125 g/4½ oz buckwheat
flakes

125 g/4½ oz rice flakes

125 g/4½ oz millet flakes

115 g/4 oz no-soak dried
apple, roughly chopped

115 g/4 oz dried stoned
dates, roughly chopped

Method

1 Heat a non-stick frying pan over a medium heat. Add the sunflower seeds, pumpkin seeds and hazelnuts and lightly toast, shaking the pan frequently, for 4 minutes, or until golden brown. Transfer to a large bowl and leave to cool.

2 Add the buckwheat flakes, rice flakes, millet flakes, apple and dates to the bowl and mix thoroughly until combined. Store the muesli in an airtight jar or container.

DATE &
CHIA PUDDING

Serves: 2   **Prep: 10 mins**   **Cook: 10 mins**

Ingredients

3 tbsp chia seeds

225 ml/8 fl oz coconut milk

½ tbsp date syrup

seeds from ½ vanilla pod

3 tbsp coconut soya yogurt

1 large medjool date,
chopped

½ orange, sliced

1 tbsp pomegranate seeds

Method

1 Place the chia seeds, coconut milk, date syrup,
and vanilla seeds in a large bowl. Stir thoroughly
to combine. Tip into a covered container and
leave to soak overnight in the refrigerator.

2 When ready to serve, divide the chia mixture into
serving bowls. Spread the coconut yogurt over
the top of each pudding, then top with the date,
orange slices and pomegranate seeds.

3 Serve immediately.

BREAKFASTS & JUICES

BUCKWHEAT & ALMOND PORRIDGE

Serves: 6

Prep: 15–20 mins **Cook: none**
plus soaking & chilling

Ingredients

Almond milk

70 g/2½ oz whole raw almonds, soaked overnight in water

300 ml/10 fl oz water

Porridge

350 g/12 oz raw buckwheat groats, soaked in cold water for 90 minutes

1 tsp cinnamon

2 tbsp light agave nectar

freshly sliced strawberries, to serve

a drizzle of honey, to serve

Method

1 To make the almond milk, drain the almonds and transfer to a blender or food processor. Blend the almonds with the water. Keep the blender running for a minute or two to break down the almonds as much as possible.

2 Pour the mixture into a sieve lined with muslin and squeeze through as much of the liquid as possible into a large bowl or jug. You should get approximately 300 ml/10 fl oz of raw almond milk.

3 Rinse the soaked buckwheat thoroughly in cold water. Transfer to the blender or food processor with the almond milk, cinnamon and agave nectar. Blend to a slightly coarse texture.

4 Chill the mixture for at least 30 minutes or overnight. It can be stored, covered, in the refrigerator for 3 days.

5 Serve in small bowls topped with the strawberries and a drizzle of honey, if liked.

MILLET PORRIDGE WITH APRICOT PURÉE

Serves: 4　　　　**Prep: 5 mins**　　　　**Cook: 30 mins**

Ingredients

225 g/8 oz millet flakes
450 ml/15 fl oz soya milk
pinch of salt

Apricot purée

115 g/4 oz dried apricots,
roughly chopped
300 ml/10 fl oz water

Method

1 To make the apricot purée, put the apricots into a saucepan and cover with the water. Bring to the boil, then reduce the heat and simmer, half covered, for 20 minutes until the apricots are very tender. Use a hand-held blender or transfer the apricots, along with any water left in the saucepan, to a food processor or blender and process until smooth. Set aside.

2 To make the porridge, put the millet flakes into a saucepan and add the milk and salt. Bring to the boil, then reduce the heat and simmer for 5 minutes, stirring frequently, until cooked and creamy.

3 To serve, spoon into four bowls and top with the apricot purée.

PEACHY TOFU FOOL

Serves: 4 **Prep: 20–25 mins** **Cook: no cook**

Ingredients

4 peaches or nectarines, stoned

3 tbsp orange juice

350 g/12 oz pack soft silken tofu, drained

2 tbsp maple syrup

40 g/1½ oz walnut pieces, roughly chopped

1 tbsp demerara sugar

Method

1 Roughly chop the peaches and purée with a hand blender or in a food processor until smooth. Add the orange juice and blend again.

2 Whizz the tofu with a hand blender or in a food processor until smooth. Stir in the maple syrup.

3 Place alternate tablespoonfuls of the fruit purée and tofu mixture into four tall glasses, or individual dishes, swirling lightly for a marbled effect.

4 Mix together the walnuts and demerara, and spoon on top of the fools just before serving.

SMASHED AVOCADO WITH TOASTED HEMP SEEDS

Serves: 2   **Prep: 5 mins**   **Cook: 1–2 mins**

Ingredients

2 tbsp raw hemp seeds

2 ripe avocados, roughly chopped

1 tbsp lemon juice

½ tbsp extra virgin olive oil

1 large garlic clove, crushed

½ tsp sea salt

½ tsp pepper

2 thick slices of gluten-free wholegrain bread, about 45 g/1¾ oz each

½ fresh red chilli, deseeded and finely chopped, to garnish

Method

1. Place a small, non-stick frying pan over a medium heat. Add the hemp seeds and toast them for 1–2 minutes, then set aside in a small dish.

2. Place the avocado in a large bowl. Add the lemon juice, oil, garlic, salt, pepper and 1½ tbsp of the toasted hemp seeds. Stir to combine, then mash to a rough purée.

3. Toast the wholegrain bread and serve the purée on the toast, sprinkled with the remaining hemp seeds and the chopped chilli.

POTATO CAKES

Serves: 4 **Prep: 20 mins** **Cook: 20–25 mins**

Ingredients

115 g/4 oz cold mashed potatoes

200 ml/7 fl oz milk

75 g/2¾ oz gluten-free self-raising flour

pinch of salt

1 egg, beaten

sunflower oil, for frying

To serve

8 good-quality bacon rashers, grilled until crisp

1½ tbsp maple syrup

Method

1 Put the mashed potatoes and milk in a food processor or blender and process to a thin purée.

2 Sift the flour and salt into a mixing bowl, make a well in the centre of the flour and add the beaten egg and potato purée. Using a balloon whisk, gradually mix the flour into the liquid ingredients, whisking well to make a smooth, creamy, fairly thick batter.

3 Heat a little oil in a large, non-stick frying pan. Pour a tablespoonful of batter per cake into the pan – you will probably fit about 3 in the pan at one time. Cook each cake for 2 minutes on each side until golden brown. Remove from the pan and keep warm while you cook the remaining potato cakes.

4 Divide the cakes between 4 warmed plates, top each serving with 2 bacon rashers and drizzle with maple syrup.

COCOA WAFFLES WITH RASPBERRIES

Serves: 6　　　**Prep: 20 mins**　　　**Cook: 30 mins**

Ingredients

5 large eggs, separated

pinch of salt

1 tbsp pure, dark
cocoa powder

40 g/1½ oz caster sugar

50 g/1¾ oz unsalted butter,
melted and cooled slightly

250 ml/8½ fl oz
semi-skimmed milk

225 g/8 oz gluten-free
plain flour

1 tbsp olive oil, for brushing

To serve

150 g/5½ oz
Greek-style yogurt

200 g/7 oz fresh raspberries

6 tbsp runny honey

Method

1　You will need an 18 cm/7 inch round waffle
maker for this recipe.

2　Place the egg yolks, salt, cocoa powder
and sugar in a medium-sized bowl and
beat well with a wooden spoon. Stir in the
butter. Slowly beat in the milk until it is fully
incorporated. Gradually add the flour until
you have a thick batter.

3　In a separate bowl, whisk the egg whites until stiff
peaks form and gently fold them into the batter.
Gently combine the mixture.

4　Heat the waffle maker according to
manufacturer's instructions. Brush the iron with
the olive oil and spoon the mixture in. Do not
overfill. Cook for 4–5 minutes and serve topped
with yogurt, raspberries and honey.

POACHED EGGS WITH TOMATO & RED PEPPER

Serves: 3–4   **Prep: 20 mins**   **Cook: 30–35 mins**

Ingredients

2 tbsp olive oil, for oiling

1 red chilli, deseeded and finely chopped

1 onion, finely chopped

3 red peppers, deseeded and sliced into thin strips

4 garlic cloves, roughly chopped

1 tsp ground cumin

1 tsp ground turmeric

¼ tsp saffron

1 x 400 g/14 oz can chopped tomatoes

3 eggs

2 tbsp roughly chopped fresh flat-leaf parsley, to garnish

4 tbsp natural yogurt, to serve

Method

1. In a deep frying pan with a lid, heat the oil until hot and add the red chilli and onion. Sizzle for 2–3 minutes, until the onion has begun to soften. Add the peppers, garlic and spices. Maintain the heat and continue to fry, covered, for 10–12 minutes. You want the peppers to be soft but not charred.

2. Pour the tomatoes into the frying pan and continue to simmer for a further 8 minutes, uncovered, until the mixture has thickened slightly.

3. Using a spoon, shape three holes in your peppe mixture and crack one egg into each hole (or if using a smaller pan, create one hole and a single egg per serving). The white may seep onto the surface of the mixture. Cover the pan and cook for about 10 minutes, until the yolks are just set.

4. Serve immediately, with a sprinkling of parsley and a spoonful of yogurt.

PLUM PANCAKES

Serves: 6   **Prep: 20 mins**   **Cook: 50 mins**

Ingredients

8 red plums, stoned and cut into quarters

100 ml/3½ fl oz maple syrup

1 tbsp lemon juice

1 piece star anise

200 g/7 oz gluten-free plain flour blend

1½ tsp gluten-free baking powder

2 eggs, beaten

200 ml/7 fl oz sweetened soya milk

100 g/3½ oz plain soya yogurt

1 tbsp sunflower oil, plus extra for greasing

Method

1 Place the plums, maple syrup, lemon juice and star anise in a pan and heat until almost boiling. Reduce the heat, cover and cook gently for 8–10 minutes, stirring occasionally, until tender.

2 Place the flour, baking powder, eggs, milk, yogurt and oil in a blender or food processor and blend to a smooth, bubbly batter.

3 Lightly grease a large, heavy-based frying pan or griddle pan and heat until very hot. Drop tablespoonfuls of the batter onto the pan and cook for 5–6 minutes, turning once, until golden and set. Cook in batches to make about 24 pancakes.

4 To serve, stack 4 pancakes on each plate and spoon over the plums and juices.

BANANA CRÊPES

Serves: 4

Prep: 20–25 mins
plus resting & standing

Cook: 30 mins

Ingredients

50 g/1¾ oz
buckwheat flour

50 g/1¾ oz gluten-free
plain flour

pinch of salt

1 large egg, lightly beaten

125 ml/4 fl oz milk

125 ml/4 fl oz water

40 g/1½ oz butter
or margarine

Maple syrup bananas

40 g/1½ oz butter
or margarine

2 tbsp maple syrup

2 bananas, thickly sliced on
the diagonal

Method

1 Sift the flours and the salt into a mixing bowl. Make a well in the centre and add the beaten egg, milk and water. Using a balloon whisk, gradually mix the flour into the liquid ingredients. Whisk until you have a smooth batter.

2 Melt 25 g/1 oz of the butter in a small saucepan and stir it into the batter. Pour the batter into a jug, cover and leave to rest for 30 minutes.

3 Melt half the remaining butter in a medium-sized frying pan. When the pan is hot, pour in enough batter to make a thin crêpe, swirling the pan to achieve an even layer.

4 Cook one side until lightly browned, then, using a palette knife, turn over and cook the other side. Slide onto a warm plate and cover with foil while you cook the remaining crêpes, adding more butter when needed.

5 To make the maple syrup bananas, wipe the frying pan, add the butter and heat until melted. Stir in the maple syrup, then add the bananas and cook for 2–3 minutes, or until the bananas have just softened and the sauce has thickened and caramelized. To serve, fold the crêpes in half and half again, then top with the bananas.

BUBBLE & SQUEAK BREAKFAST BOWL

Serves: 2   **Prep: 5 mins**   **Cook: 10 mins**

Ingredients

400 g/14 oz sweet potato, peeled and cut into chunks

200 g/7 oz kale, chopped

2 eggs

2 tsp coconut oil

1 tsp cumin seeds

1 tsp mustard seeds

1 tsp pepper

½ tsp ground turmeric

25 g/1 oz walnuts, chopped

25 g/1 oz blanched almonds, chopped

25 g/1 oz pumpkin seeds

Method

1 Place the sweet potato in a steamer and cook for 5–6 minutes, until tender. Add the kale to the steamer for the last 2 minutes of cooking.

2 Meanwhile, bring a small saucepan of water to the boil, break the eggs into a cup, one at a time, add to the pan and poach for 4–5 minutes.

3 Heat the oil in a large frying pan or wok and add the cumin seeds, mustard seeds, pepper and turmeric. Cook until the mustard seeds begin to 'pop', then add the steamed vegetables and toss.

4 Divide the spiced vegetables between two warmed bowls and top each one with a poached egg.

5 Sprinkle each serving with walnuts, almonds and pumpkin seeds and serve immediately.

★ Variation

Other root vegetables such as parsnip or swede could also be used, and the kale could be substituted with spring greens or cabbage – choose your favourite vegetables for this one!

FLUFFY PANCAKES WITH BLUEBERRIES & ALMONDS

Makes: 12–14   **Prep: 20 mins**   **Cook: 15 mins**

Ingredients

5 eggs, separated

175 g/6 oz gluten-free plain flour

1½ tsp gluten-free baking powder

pinch of salt

150 ml/5 fl oz semi-skimmed milk

1 tbsp olive oil, for oiling

To serve

70 g/2½ oz flaked almonds, toasted

60 ml/2 fl oz agave syrup

100 g/3½ oz blueberries

Method

1 Mix the egg yolks with the flour, baking powder and salt. Stir in the milk.

2 Whisk the egg whites and delicately fold them into the mixture until combined.

3 Heat the oil in a heavy-based frying pan and drop spoonfuls of the batter into the hot pan. Heat for about 1 minute, or until bubbles start to form, and use a spatula to turn over and cook the other side. Remove the pancakes from the pan and keep them warm in the oven.

4 Serve the pancakes topped with the almonds, agave syrup and blueberries.

★ Variation

If you have a sweet tooth, add a dash of vanilla essence to the batter for heavenly vanilla pancakes.

BAKED EGGS WITH ASPARAGUS

Serves: 2   **Prep: 10 mins**   **Cook: 12 mins**

Ingredients

1¼ tbsp extra virgin rapeseed oil

½ tsp paprika

1 garlic clove, crushed

¼ tsp sea salt

¼ tsp pepper

12 asparagus spears, woody ends removed

4 eggs

1 tomato, deseeded and diced

1 tbsp snipped fresh chives

Method

1 Preheat the oven to 190°C/375°F/Gas Mark 5. In a small bowl, combine 1 tablespoon of the oil with all but a pinch of the paprika. Thoroughly stir in the garlic, salt and pepper.

2 Coat the asparagus spears thoroughly in the flavoured oil then place in two shallow gratin dishes. Roast in the preheated oven for 7 minutes, or until nearly tender when pierced with a sharp knife.

3 Crack the eggs evenly over the asparagus and drizzle over any remaining seasoned oil. Return to the oven for 5 minutes, or until the whites are set and the yolks still runny.

4 Serve the eggs and asparagus with the diced tomatoes and chives sprinkled over the top. Drizzle with the remaining rapeseed oil and garnish with the remaining pinch of paprika.

SAUSAGE & EGG SIZZLE

Serves: 4　　　**Prep: 20 mins**　　　**Cook: 35–40 mins**

Ingredients

4 gluten-free sausages or vegetarian alternative

sunflower oil, for frying

4 peeled and boiled potatoes, cooled and diced

8 cherry tomatoes

4 eggs, beaten

salt and pepper (optional)

Method

1　Preheat the grill to medium–high. Arrange the sausages on a foil-lined grill pan and cook under the preheated grill, turning occasionally, for 12–15 minutes, or until cooked through and golden brown. Leave to cool slightly, then slice into bite-sized pieces.

2　Meanwhile, heat a little oil in a medium-sized (25 cm/10 inch), heavy-based frying pan with a heatproof handle over a medium heat. Add the potatoes and cook until golden brown and crisp all over, then add the tomatoes and cook for a further 2 minutes. Arrange the sausages in the pan so that there is an even distribution of potatoes, tomatoes and sausages.

3　Add a little more oil to the pan if it seems dry. Season the beaten eggs to taste, if using salt and pepper, and pour the mixture over the ingredients in the pan. Cook for 3 minutes, without stirring or disturbing the eggs. Place the pan under the preheated grill for 3 minutes, or until the top is just cooked. Cut into wedges to serve.

POTATO & ONION FRITTATA

Serves: 4　　　　**Prep: 15 mins**　　　　**Cook: 60 mins**

Ingredients

4 tbsp olive oil

2 large onions, halved and thinly sliced

125 ml/4 fl oz water

50 g/1¾ oz red quinoa, rinsed

700 g/1 lb 9 oz waxy potatoes, peeled, halved lengthways and thinly sliced

9 eggs

½ tsp dried oregano

½ tsp salt

½ tsp pepper

Method

1　Heat the oil in a frying pan, add the onions and gently fry over a low–medium heat for 25 minutes, until golden and very soft. Drain the onions, reserving the oil.

2　Meanwhile, put the water and quinoa into a small saucepan and bring to the boil. Cover and simmer over a very low heat for 10 minutes, or until most of the liquid has evaporated. Remove from the heat, but leave the pan covered for a further 10 minutes to allow the grains to swell. Fluff up with a fork.

3　While the quinoa is cooking, put the potatoes in a steamer and steam for 8 minutes, until just tender. Spread out to dry on a clean tea towel.

4　Beat the eggs with the oregano, and salt and pepper. Stir the onions, potatoes and quinoa into the egg mixture.

5　Heat the reserved oil in a deep 25 cm/10 inch non-stick frying pan. Pour in the egg mixture, cover and cook over a low–medium heat for 15 minutes. Meanwhile, preheat the grill.

6　Place the pan under the preheated grill for 5 minutes to finish cooking the top of the frittata. Turn out onto a plate, cut into wedges and serve immediately.

BREAKFAST MUFFINS

Makes: 12

Prep: 20–25 mins
plus cooling

Cook: 20 mins

Ingredients

300 g/10½ oz gluten-free plain white flour blend

4 tsp gluten-free baking powder

½ tsp xanthan gum

1 tsp ground mixed spice

140 g/5 oz light muscovado sugar

40 g/1½ oz sunflower seeds

175 g/6 oz grated carrots

finely grated rind and juice 1 small orange

2 eggs, beaten

150 ml/5 fl oz milk

100 ml/3½ fl oz sunflower oil

1 tsp vanilla extract

Method

1 Preheat the oven to 200°C/400°F/Gas Mark 6. Place 12 paper muffin cases into a deep muffin tray.

2 Sift the flour, baking powder, xanthan gum and mixed spice into a large bowl. Stir in the sugar with 25 g/1 oz sunflower seeds, carrots and orange rind.

3 Lightly beat together the orange juice, eggs, milk, oil and vanilla with a fork and stir into the dry ingredients, mixing to make a rough batter.

4 Spoon the batter into the muffin cases and sprinkle with the remaining sunflower seeds. Bake in the oven for about 20 minutes, or until well risen and golden brown. Serve warm.

BLUEBERRY BARS

Makes: 12

Prep: 20 mins
plus cooling

Cook: 30–35 mins

Ingredients

sunflower oil, for greasing

85 g/3 oz gluten-free
self-raising flour

55 g/2 oz quinoa flakes

55 g/2 oz puffed rice

55 g/2 oz flaked almonds

225 g/8 oz blueberries

100 g/3½ oz butter

100 g/3½ oz honey

1 egg, beaten

Method

1 Preheat the oven to 180°C/350°F/Gas Mark 4. Grease a 28 x 18 cm/11 x 7 inch traybake tin and line the base with non-stick baking paper.

2 Mix together the flour, quinoa, puffed rice, almonds and blueberries. Place the butter and honey in a pan and heat gently until just melted, then stir evenly into the dry ingredients with the egg.

3 Spread the mixture into the prepared tin, smoothing with a palette knife. Bake in the oven for 25–30 minutes, until golden brown and firm.

4 Leave to cool in the tin for 15 minutes, and cut into 12 bars. Transfer to a wire rack to continue cooling.

BREAKFAST CEREAL BARS

Makes: 12   **Prep: 10 mins**   **Cook: 30–35 mins**

Ingredients

100 g/3½ oz butter, softened, plus extra for greasing

30 g/1 oz light muscovado sugar

2 tbsp golden syrup

2 eggs, beaten

100 g/3½ oz millet flakes

70 g/2½ oz raisins

55 g/2 oz quinoa

50 g/1¾ oz dried cranberries

70 g/2½ oz sultanas

25 g/1 oz pumpkin seeds

25 g/1 oz sesame seeds

25 g/1 oz chopped walnuts

35 g/1¼ oz desiccated coconut

Method

1 Preheat the oven to 180°C/350°F/Gas Mark 4. Grease a 25 x 18 cm/10 x 7 inch baking tray and line it with baking paper.

2 Beat together the butter, sugar and syrup until creamy in a large bowl. Add all the remaining ingredients and stir well until combined.

3 Place the mixture in the tin and level the surface with a spatula or palette knife.

4 Bake in the preheated oven for 30–35 mins or until golden brown.

5 When cool, turn out onto a flat surface and cut into 12 bars. The bars can be stored in an airtight container for up to 1 week.

LAYERED POWERBOWL SMOOTHIE

Serves: 2   **Prep: 12 mins**   **Cook: none**

Ingredients

1 large mango, peeled and chopped

2 kiwi fruit, peeled and chopped

½ tsp chlorella powder

450 g/1 lb watermelon, peeled and chopped (leave the pips in for additional vitamins)

1 tbsp ground almonds

1 tsp sesame seeds

2 tbsp granola

¼ tsp ground cinnamon

Method

1 Place the mango in a small blender and process until smooth. Divide between two glass bowls. Rinse the blender.

2 Place the kiwi and chlorella powder in the blender and process until smooth. Spoon over the layer of mango in the bowls. Rinse the blender.

3 Place the watermelon in the blender and process until smooth. Add the ground almonds and sesame seeds and process briefly to combine. Spoon over the kiwi mixture.

4 Sprinkle with the granola and ground cinnamon and serve.

★ Variation

Ground nuts or seeds can be added to any of the fruit layers here to thicken them and add extra nutrients – try some ground golden linseeds in the mango for additional essential fats and fibre.

VANILLA, ALMOND & BANANA SMOOTHIE

Serves: 2   **Prep: 5 mins**   **Cook: none**

Ingredients

225 ml/8 fl oz almond milk
50 g/2¼ oz almond butter
1 banana, sliced
4 stoned dates
1 tsp vanilla extract
8–10 ice cubes

Method

1 Place all of the ingredients in a blender and blend on high speed until smooth.

2 Pour into two glasses and serve immediately.

TANTALIZING TOMATO JUICE

Serves: 1   **Prep: 5 mins**   **Cook: none**

Ingredients

2 carrots, halved

1 celery stalk, halved

2.5-cm/1-inch slice
of broccoli stem

6 basil leaves, plus a sprig
to decorate

4 tomatoes

small handful of ice
(optional)

Method

1 Feed the carrots, then the celery, broccoli
and the basil, and finally the tomatoes through
a juicer.

2 Fill a glass halfway with ice, if using, then pour in
the juice. Garnish with the basil sprig and serve
immediately.

STRAWBERRY & VANILLA SOYA SHAKE

Serves: 2 **Prep: 10–15 mins** **Cook: none**

Ingredients

200 g/7 oz strawberries

200 ml/7 fl oz plain soya yogurt

100 ml/3½ fl oz chilled soya milk

2 tsp vanilla extract

Method

1 Pick over the strawberries, then hull and halve them and place into a small bowl.

2 Place the strawberry halves, yogurt, milk and vanilla extract into a food processor or blender, or place these ingredients into a large, deep bowl and use a hand-held blender. Blend gently until thoroughly combined.

3 Serve immediately in tall drinking glasses.

BREAKFASTS & JUICES

SNACKS & LIGHT BITES

HOT SALAMI & QUINOA WITH GARLIC MAYO

Makes: 15–20　　　　**Prep: 25 mins**　　　　**Cook: 20 mins**

Ingredients

500 g/1 lb 2 oz cooked quinoa

50 g/1¾ oz gluten-free plain flour

50 g/1¾ oz sun-dried tomatoes, roughly chopped

3 tbsp chopped fresh parsley

25 g/1 oz freshly grated Parmesan cheese

2 eggs, lightly beaten

3 tbsp sunflower oil, for oiling

6 thin slices gluten-free salami, cut into strips

salt and pepper (optional)

Garlic mayonnaise

70 g/2½ oz gluten-free mayonnaise

½ tsp smoked paprika

1 garlic clove, crushed

Method

1. To make the garlic mayonnaise, combine the mayonnaise, paprika and garlic in a small bowl and set aside.

2. Start making the bites. Put the quinoa, flour, sun-dried tomatoes, 2 tablespoons of the parsley and the cheese in a large bowl and combine with the beaten eggs. Season to taste with salt and pepper, if using.

3. Form the mixture into 15–20 small patties using your hands and place on a tray lined with kitchen paper.

4. Heat the sunflower oil in a large non-stick pan. In batches, cook the patties on each side for 3–5 minutes, or until they are golden brown. Once cooked, leave to rest on a tray lined with kitchen paper.

5. In the same pan, fry the salami until it is crispy and beginning to curl.

6. Serve the quinoa bites topped with half a teaspoon of the garlic mayonnaise, the crispy salami and any remaining parsley.

BEAN, CRUNCHY CABBAGE & CARROT TACOS

Serves: 4   **Prep: 30 mins**   **Cook: 45–55 mins**

Ingredients

2 tbsp olive oil

1 garlic clove, crushed

200 g/7 oz canned
chopped tomatoes

1 tsp smoked paprika

1 tsp brown sugar

1 x 400 g/14 oz can pinto
beans, drained and rinsed

¼ small red cabbage,
shredded

½ red onion, shredded

2 ripe tomatoes,
roughly chopped

juice of 1 lime

salt and pepper (optional)

3 tbsp soured cream,
to serve

Taco shells

400 g/14 oz carrots, grated

50 g/1¾ oz strong, mature
Cheddar cheese, grated

50 g/1¾ oz gluten-free
plain flour

1 egg, beaten

salt and pepper (optional)

Method

1 Preheat the oven to 200°C/400°F/Gas Mark 6.

2 To make the taco shells, steam the carrots in a medium-sized steamer for 10 minutes, or until they are tender. Drain the carrots and place in a tea towel or square of muslin. Firmly squeeze out all of the excess liquid.

3 In a medium-sized bowl, combine the carrot with the cheese, flour and egg. Season to taste with salt and pepper, if using.

4 Line a large baking tray with baking paper and divide the shell mixture into golf ball-sized portions. Space the portions out on the tray and press down with the palm of your hand until you have 4 flat rounds, roughly 14–15 cm/ 5½–6 inches in diameter.

5 Cook the shells in the preheated oven for 15–20 minutes, or until they begin to brown. Once cooked, tear away the baking paper and gently bend the sides or mould the shells around a glass to form a taco shape. Allow the shells to cool before filling them.

6 To prepare the filling, heat 1 tablespoon of the olive oil in a small saucepan over a medium heat and gently fry the garlic for 2–3 minutes.

7 Add the tomatoes, paprika and sugar to the pan, bring to the boil and reduce to a simmer for 10–15 minutes. Add the beans and cook for a further 5 minutes. Season to taste with salt and pepper, if using.

8 Combine the red cabbage, red onion and tomatoes in a bowl. Dress with the lime juice and the remaining oil. Spoon the bean mixture into the taco shells and top with the cabbage mixture. Serve the tacos drizzled with soured cream.

SALMON DEVILLED EGGS WITH BLACK ONION SEEDS

Makes: 16 halves   **Prep: 15 mins**   **Cook: 8 mins**

Ingredients

8 large eggs

50 ml/1¾ fl oz gluten-free mayonnaise

50 ml/1¾ fl oz crème fraîche

2 tsp gluten-free Dijon mustard

40 g/1½ oz smoked salmon, sliced into small pieces

15 g/½ oz fresh dill, chopped

1 tbsp black onion seeds

salt and pepper (optional)

Method

1 In a large saucepan, cover the eggs with cold water. Bring to the boil over a high heat, then reduce to a simmer and cook for 8 minutes. Strain and immediately place the eggs in fresh cold water.

2 Once cooled, peel and slice the eggs in half. Scoop out the cooked yolk and combine in a bowl with the mayonnaise, crème fraîche, mustard, salmon and half of the dill. Season to taste with salt and pepper, if using.

3 Spoon the yolk mixture into the egg whites and serve topped with the remaining dill and the onion seeds.

PRAWN & MANGO WITH CUCUMBER SALAD

Serves: 4 **Prep: 20 mins** **Cook: 10 mins**

Ingredients

200 g/7 oz raw prawns, peeled and deveined

1 mango, peeled, stoned and cut into 2-cm/¾-inch chunks

2 tsp finely chopped fresh coriander

zest of 1 lime

1 tbsp olive oil, for oiling

Cucumber salad

1 cucumber, sliced

½ red chilli, deseeded and finely diced

2 tbsp roughly chopped fresh coriander

2 spring onions, roughly chopped

juice of 1 lime

Method

1 If you'd like to serve the dish on skewers, prepare them by soaking them in warm water for 10–30 minutes – this will stop the skewers from cooking with the food.

2 Mix the prawns and mango in a medium-sized bowl and add the coriander and lime zest. Leave to marinate for 10 minutes.

3 Meanwhile, make the cucumber salad. Put all of the ingredients in a bowl and lightly toss them together.

4 Heat the olive oil in a griddle pan over a high heat. Thread the prawn and mango onto skewers, if using, and cook on both sides for 3–4 minutes, until lightly charred.

5 Serve the prawn and mango with the fresh cucumber salad, leaving the skewers to serve, if preferred.

MIXED SEED CRACKERS

Makes: 30

Prep: 10 mins

Cook: 1 hour 20 mins

Ingredients

85 g/3 oz chia seeds

85 g/3 oz golden linseeds

250 ml/9 fl oz cold water

85 g/3 oz pumpkin seeds

85 g/3 oz sunflower seeds

2 tbsp ground linseed
with berries

1 tbsp sesame seeds

1 tsp sea salt

2 tsp nutritional yeast flakes

½ tsp dried rosemary

½ tsp dried thyme

Method

1 Put the chia seeds and golden linseeds in a large bowl. Tip in the water, stir and set aside for 15 minutes. Preheat the oven to 140°C/275°F/ Gas Mark 1.

2 Stir in the other ingredients and mix to combine. Line a baking tray that is approximately 28 x 38 cm/11 x 15 inches with baking paper. Tip the mixture onto the baking paper and spread it out evenly across the tray – use your clean fingers or the back of a large spoon to do this.

3 When the mixture is spread evenly, make four evenly spaced lengthways scores into the top half of the mix. Make five evenly spaced crossways scores so that you have an outline for 30 rectangular crackers. Place the baking tray in the centre of the oven and bake for 45 minutes.

4 Take the tray out and turn the cracker sheet over using two large flat spatulas. (You can also cut the cracker sheet into two down one of the scores, using a large sharp knife, before turning) Return to the oven for 35 minutes.

5 Turn the cracker sheet out onto a wooden board and, while still warm, cut into 30 crackers through the score marks. Place on a wire rack to cool for at least 30 minutes, then serve or store in an airtight container.

SNACKS & LIGHT BITES

ROOT VEG CRISPS WITH YOGURT DIP

Serves: 4 **Prep: 30 mins** **Cook: 16 mins, plus cooling**

Ingredients

1 kg/2 lb 4 oz mixed root vegetables, such as carrots, parsnips or sweet potatoes and golden beetroot, very thinly sliced

4 tbsp virgin olive oil

sea salt and pepper (optional)

Herby garlic dip

200 g/7 oz Greek-style natural yogurt

2 garlic cloves, finely chopped

4 tbsp finely chopped fresh herbs, such as flat-leaf parsley, chives, basil and oregano

Method

1 Preheat the oven to 200°C/400°F/Gas Mark 6. To make the herby garlic dip, spoon the yogurt into a jug, then stir in the garlic and herbs and season with salt and pepper, if using. Cover and chill in the refrigerator.

2 Put the vegetables in a large bowl. Slowly drizzle over the oil, gently turning the vegetables as you go, until they are all coated.

3 Arrange the vegetables over three baking sheets in a single layer, then season with salt and pepper, if using. Bake for 8–10 minutes then check – the slices in the corners of the trays will cook more quickly, so transfer any that are crisp and golden to a wire rack. Cook the rest for 2–3 minutes more, then transfer any more cooked crisps to the wire rack. Cook the remaining slices for 2–3 minutes more if needed, then transfer to the wire rack and leave to cool.

4 Arrange the crisps in a bowl and spoon the dip into a smaller bowl, then serve.

SPICED BEETROOT & CUCUMBER TZATZIKI

Serves: 4   **Prep: 10–15 mins**   **Cook: none**

Ingredients

115 g/4 oz cooked beetroot in natural juices, drained and diced (drained weight)

150 g/5½ oz cucumber, diced

40 g/1½ oz radishes, diced

1 spring onion, finely chopped

12 Little Gem lettuce leaves

Dressing

150 g/5½ oz 2 per cent fat Greek-style natural yogurt

¼ tsp ground cumin

½ tsp runny honey

2 tbsp finely chopped fresh mint

salt and pepper (optional)

Method

1 To make the dressing, put the yogurt, cumin and honey in a bowl, then stir in the mint and season to taste with salt and pepper, if using.

2 Add the beetroot, cucumber, radishes and spring onion, then toss gently together.

3 Arrange the lettuce leaves on a plate. Spoon a little of the salad into each leaf. Serve immediately.

ROAST KALE CRISPS

Serves: 4   **Prep: 15 mins**   **Cook: 15 mins**

Ingredients

250 g/9 oz kale

2 tbsp olive oil

2 pinches of sugar

2 pinches of sea salt

2 tbsp toasted flaked
almonds, to garnish

Method

1. Preheat the oven to 150°C/300°F/Gas Mark 2. Remove the thick stems and central rib from the kale (leaving about 125 g/4½ oz trimmed leaves). Rinse and dry very thoroughly with kitchen paper. Tear into bite-sized pieces and place in a bowl with the oil and sugar, then toss well.

2. Spread about half the leaves in a single layer in a large roasting tin, spaced well apart. Sprinkle with a pinch of sea salt and roast on the bottom rack of the preheated oven for 4 minutes.

2. Stir the leaves, then turn the tray so the back is at the front. Roast for a further 1–2 minutes, until the leaves are crisp and very slightly browned at the edges. Repeat with the remaining leaves and sea salt. Sprinkle the kale crisps with the flaked almonds and serve immediately.

SNACKS & LIGHT BITES

FLAVOURED QUINOA BALLS

Makes: 24   **Prep: 35 mins**   **Cook: 35 mins**

Ingredients

115 g/4 oz quinoa

350 ml/12 fl oz boiling water

3 tomatoes, halved

2 garlic cloves, finely chopped

2 tsp torn fresh thyme leaves

2 tbsp virgin olive oil

115 g/4 oz young spinach leaves, rinsed

175 g/6 oz feta cheese, finely grated (drained weight)

pinch of grated nutmeg

25 g/1 oz stoned black olives, finely chopped

1 tbsp chopped fresh basil

sea salt and pepper (optional)

Method

1 Add the quinoa and water to a medium-sized saucepan, cover and cook over a medium heat for about 20 minutes, stirring occasionally until the quinoa is soft and has absorbed all the water.

2 Meanwhile, preheat the grill. Arrange the tomatoes, cut-side up, on the base of a foil-lined grill rack. Sprinkle with the garlic, thyme and a little salt and pepper, if using, then drizzle with 1 tablespoon of the oil and grill for 10 minutes.

3 Add the spinach to a dry, non-stick frying pan and cook for 2–3 minutes, until just wilted. Scoop out of the pan and finely chop, then mix with one third of the quinoa, one third of the cheese, a little nutmeg, and salt and pepper to taste, if using.

4 Peel the tomatoes, chop and add with any pan juices to the empty spinach pan. Stir in half the remaining quinoa and cook for 2–3 minutes, until the mixture is dry enough to shape into a ball. Remove from the heat and stir in half the remaining cheese.

5 Mix the remaining quinoa and cheese with the olives, basil and a little salt and pepper, if using. Shape each of the flavoured quinoa mixtures into 8 small balls. Chill until ready to serve.

6 Preheat the oven to 180°C/350°F/Gas Mark 4. Brush a roasting tin with the remaining oil, add the quinoa balls and bake for 10 minutes, turning once, until the edges are golden brown and the cheese has melted. Serve hot or cold. Transfer the cooled quinoa balls to an airtight container, refrigerate and eat within 2–3 days.

CARROT & CASHEW PÂTÉ ON CRACKERS

Serves: 4   **Prep: 5 mins**   **Cook: none**

Ingredients

140 g/5 oz raw cashew nuts, soaked in cold water overnight, or for at least 4 hours

300 g/10½ oz carrots, chopped

55 g/2 oz light gluten-free tahini

juice of 1 lemon

2 tsp finely chopped fresh ginger

1 large garlic clove, crushed

½ tsp sea salt

2 tbsp chopped fresh coriander leaves

50 g/1¾ oz microsalad leaves, to serve

8 gluten-free mixed seed crackers, to serve

Method

1 Drain the cashew nuts thoroughly.

2 Place all of the ingredients, except the fresh coriander leaves, in an electric food processor or blender. Process until you have a smooth mixture.

3 Stir the coriander leaves into the mixture and spoon into 8-cm/3¼-inch round ramekins. Cover with clingfilm and chill for 2 hours before serving.

4 Spread the pâté onto the crackers and serve immediately with the microsalad leaves.

SPRING ROLLS

Makes: 16 rolls

Prep: 25–30 mins
plus marinating

Cook: 15–20 mins

Ingredients

2 tbsp gluten-free tamari

1½ tsp maple syrup

500 g/1 lb 2 oz lean pork fillets

vegetable oil, for frying

32 rice paper pancakes

gluten-free hoisin sauce

70 g/2½ oz rice vermicelli noodles, cooked

strips of cucumber

strips of spring onion

Method

1 Blend the tamari and maple syrup together in a shallow dish. Add the pork and turn to coat in the mixture. Cover and leave to marinate in the refrigerator for at least 1 hour or preferably overnight.

2 Heat a griddle pan over a medium–high heat until hot, add a little oil to cover the base and cook the pork for 4–6 minutes each side, depending on the thickness of the fillets, until cooked and caramelized on the outside. Remove from the pan and slice into fine strips.

3 Fill a heatproof bowl with water that is just off the boil. Put 2 rice paper pancakes on top of one another (you will need 2 per roll as they are very thin and fragile) and soak in the water for 20 seconds, or until they turn pliable and opaque. Carefully remove using a spatula, drain for a second and place flat on a plate.

4 Spread a spoonful of hoisin sauce over the pancake and top with a small bundle of noodles and a few strips of pork, cucumber and spring onion. Fold in the ends and sides of the pancake to resemble a spring roll. Set aside while you make the remaining rolls. Slice in half on the diagonal and serve with a little more hoisin sauce, if liked.

HONEY & SPICE SNACKING NUTS

Serves: 6   **Prep: 5–10 mins**   **Cook: 10 mins**

Ingredients

75 g/2¾ oz Brazil nuts
50 g/1¾ oz pecan nuts
50 g/1¾ oz cashew nuts
25 g/1 oz pumpkin seeds
1 tbsp sunflower oil
1½ tbsp runny honey
½ tsp ground cinnamon
½ tsp mixed spice
½ tsp black pepper
½ tsp sweet paprika
¼ tsp salt

Method

1 Line a baking tray with baking parchment. Preheat the oven to 140°C/275°F/Gas Mark 1.

2 Combine all the ingredients in a bowl, except for half a tablespoon of the honey, and then spread out onto the prepared baking tray.

3 Place onto the middle shelf of the oven and cook for 10 minutes. Remove from the oven and drizzle the remaining honey over the nuts. Leave to cool, then serve. Store in an airtight container for up to a week.

SNACKS & LIGHT BITES

FIBRE-RICH FRUIT & TRAIL MIX

Serves: 20–25   **Prep: 10 mins**   **Cook: 8-10 mins**

Ingredients

200 g/7 oz whole
unblanched almonds

25 g/1 oz pine nuts

5 g/1 oz pumpkin seeds

g/1 oz sunflower seeds

25 g/1 oz dried banana
chips

55 g/2 oz dates, stoned
and roughly chopped

2 tbsp oat bran

tsp ground mixed spice

1 small egg white

Method

1 Preheat the oven to 200°C/400°F/Gas Mark 6.
Combine the almonds, pine nuts, pumpkin and
sunflower seeds, banana chips, dates, oat bran
and spice in a large bowl and mix well.

2 Lightly beat the egg white with a fork in a small
bowl, then add to the nut mixture in the bowl,
stirring to coat all the ingredients evenly.

3 Spread the mixture out on a large baking sheet
in a single layer. Bake in the preheated oven for
8–10 minutes, or until crisp and lightly browned.

4 Leave to cool completely before serving or pack
into an airtight container and consume within
5 days.

SNACKS & LIGHT BITES

NUTTY TOFFEE POPCORN

Serves: 2   **Prep: 5–10 mins**   **Cook: 10–15 mins**

Ingredients

40 g/1½ oz butter
40 g/1½ oz brown sugar
1 tbsp golden syrup
70 g/2½ oz cashew nuts
50 g/1¾ oz popping corn
1 tbsp vegetable oil

Method

1 Place the margarine, sugar and golden syrup in a saucepan over a medium heat. Bring the temperature up to high and stir continuously for 2 minutes, then remove from the heat and set aside.

2 Toast the cashew nuts in a dry, heavy-based pan over a medium heat for 3–4 minutes, stirring frequently, until they begin to turn golden brown. Remove from the heat and transfer to a plate.

3 In a large, lidded saucepan, stir the popping corn together with the oil until it is well coated. Put the lid on the pan and place over a medium heat. Listen for popping and turn the heat to low. Shake the pan occasionally, holding the lid down firmly. Do not lift the lid until the popping has finished.

4 While the popcorn is still warm, stir in the toasted cashews. Pour over the toffee sauce and stir well to coat the popcorn. Transfer the popcorn to a baking sheet lined with baking paper and allow to cool before serving.

SWEET POTATO ROUNDS WITH GOAT'S CHEESE & OLIVES

Makes: 15–20   **Prep: 20 mins**   **Cook: 25–30 mins**

Ingredients

2 large sweet potatoes, peeled and cut into 1 cm/½ inch slices

2 tbsp olive oil, for oiling

1 tbsp chilli oil

100 g/3½ oz goat's cheese, crumbled

100 g/3½ oz black olives, stoned and sliced

1 tbsp snipped fresh chives

salt and pepper (optional)

Method

1 Preheat the oven to 200°C/400°F/Gas Mark 6.

2 Place the potato slices on an oiled baking sheet and brush with chilli oil, or use a baking sheet lined with greaseproof paper. Season to taste with salt and pepper, if using, and bake in the oven for 20–25 minutes, turning halfway through until the slices become crispy around the edges. Remove from the oven and reduce the temperature to 180°C/350°F/Gas Mark 4.

3 Sprinkle the rounds with goat's cheese and gently push the olives into the cheese. Return the rounds to the oven and cook for a further 5 minutes.

4 Remove the rounds and serve, garnished with the chives.

SPICED RED CABBAGE & CORIANDER CROQUETTES

Makes: 8 **Prep: 30 mins** **Cook: 30–45 mins**

Ingredients

400 g/14 oz white potatoes, peeled and cut into chunks

½ small red cabbage, shredded

2 tbsp olive oil

1 tsp cumin seeds

1 red onion, finely chopped

1 garlic clove, crushed

2 egg yolks

1 tsp ground turmeric

½ tsp hot chilli powder

½ tsp ground coriander

15 g/½ oz fresh coriander, roughly chopped

25 g/1 oz gluten-free plain flour

2 tbsp sunflower oil

salt and pepper (optional)

Method

1 Bring a large saucepan of water to the boil over a high heat. Add the potatoes, lower the heat to a simmer and cook for 15–20 minutes. Strain and allow the potatoes to steam dry.

2 Bring a medium-sized pan of water to the boil. Add the red cabbage and cook over a medium heat for 5–10 minutes, or until the cabbage is tender. Drain well and toss the cabbage in 1 tablespoon of the olive oil and the cumin seeds.

3 In a small pan, add the remaining oil over a low heat. Add the red onion and cook gently for 5–10 minutes, or until it begins to soften. Add the garlic and cook for 3 minutes. Set aside.

4 Roughly mash the potatoes, leaving some lumps. Stir through the egg yolks, spices, onion mixture and cabbage, and then the coriander. Season to taste with salt and pepper, if using.

5 Form the mixture into 8 patties and chill in the refrigerator for at least 30 minutes.

6 Lightly coat each croquette in the flour, tapping off any excess. In a large, heavy-based frying pan, heat the sunflower oil over a medium–high heat. Once hot, add the croquettes and cook each side for 5 minutes, until they turn crisp and golden brown. Serve the croquettes immediately.

CHICKEN BALLS WITH DIPPING SAUCE

Serves: 4   **Prep: 25–30 mins**   **Cook: 18–26 mins**

Ingredients

2 large skinless, boneless chicken breasts

3 tbsp vegetable oil

2 shallots, finely chopped

½ celery stick, finely chopped

1 garlic clove, crushed

2 tbsp gluten-free tamari

1 small egg, lightly beaten

1 bunch of spring onions

salt and pepper (optional)

Dipping sauce

3 tbsp tamari

1 tbsp rice wine

1 tsp sesame seeds

Method

1 Cut the chicken into 2-cm/¾-inch pieces. Heat half of the oil in a frying pan and stir-fry the chicken over a high heat for 2–3 minutes, until golden. Remove from the pan with a slotted spoon and set aside.

2 Add the shallots, celery and garlic and stir-fry for 1–2 minutes, until softened.

3 Place the chicken and vegetables in a food processor and process until finely minced. Add 1 tablespoon of tamari and enough egg to make a firm mixture. Season to taste, if using salt and pepper.

4 To make the dipping sauce, mix together the tamari, rice wine and sesame seeds in a small serving bowl and set aside.

5 Shape the chicken mixture into 16 walnut-sized balls. Heat the remaining oil in the pan and stir-fry the balls in small batches for 4–5 minutes, until golden. Drain on kitchen paper.

6 Add the spring onions to the pan and stir-fry for 1–2 minutes, until they begin to soften, then stir in the remaining tamari. Serve the chicken balls with the stir-fried spring onions and the dipping sauce.

SNACKS & LIGHT BITES

RED CABBAGE SALAD
WITH AUBERGINE DIP

Serves: 4   **Prep: 10–15 mins**   **Cook: 15–20 mins**

Ingredients

2 carrots

50 g/12 oz red cabbage,
shredded

55 g/2 oz raisins

125 g/4½ oz bistro salad
(a mix of red-stemmed
baby red chard, bull's
blood chard and
lamb's lettuce)

juice of 1 orange

pepper

Dip

3 aubergines

3 garlic cloves, finely
chopped

2 tbsp gluten-free tahini

3 tbsp hemp oil

pepper

Method

1 To make the dip, preheat the grill to high and
remove the grill rack. Prick both ends of each
aubergine with a fork, put them in the grill pan
and grill 5 cm/2 inches away from the heat
source, turning several times, for 15–20 minutes,
until blackened. Leave to cool.

2 Shave the carrots into long, thin ribbons using a
swivel-bladed vegetable peeler, then put them
on a serving plate. Add the cabbage, then
sprinkle over the raisins and salad leaves. Drizzle
with the orange juice and season with a little
pepper.

3 Cut the aubergines in half and scoop the soft
flesh away from the blackened skins using a
dessertspoon. Finely chop the flesh, then put it
in a bowl. Add the garlic, tahini and hemp oil,
season with a little pepper and mix together.
Spoon into a serving bowl and nestle in the
centre of the salad to serve.

SNACKS & LIGHT BITES

VEGETABLE PAKORAS

Serves: 4 **Prep: 30–40 mins** **Cook: 20 mins**

Ingredients

6 tbsp gram flour

½ tsp salt

1 tsp chilli powder

1 tsp gluten-free baking powder

1½ tsp white cumin seeds

1 tsp pomegranate seeds

300 ml/10 fl oz water

¼ bunch of fresh coriander, finely chopped

400 g/14 oz mixed vegetables of your choice: cauliflower, cut into small florets; onions, cut into rings and potatoes, sliced

vegetable oil, for deep frying

2 fresh coriander sprigs, to garnish

Method

1 Sift the gram flour into a large bowl. Add the salt, chilli powder, baking powder, cumin seeds and pomegranate seeds and blend together well. Pour in the water and beat well until a smooth batter forms. Add the chopped coriander and mix well, then set aside.

2 Dip the prepared vegetables into the batter, carefully shaking off any excess.

3 Heat enough oil for deep-frying in a wok, deep-fat fryer or a large, heavy-based saucepan to 180–190°C/350–375°F, or until a cube of bread browns in 30 seconds. Using tongs, place the battered vegetables in the oil and deep-fry, in batches, turning once.

4 Repeat this process until all of the batter has been used up. Transfer the fried vegetables to crumpled kitchen paper and drain thoroughly. Garnish with coriander sprigs and serve immediately.

★ **Variation**

Other vegetable options to use in the pakoras could be sliced aubergines or fresh spinach leaves.

TABBOULEH-STUFFED JALAPEÑOS

Serves: 4   **Prep: 22 mins**   **Cook: 10–12 mins**

Ingredients

75 g/2½ oz quinoa

100 g/3½ oz fresh parsley, chopped

100 g/3½ oz fresh mint, chopped

100 g/3½ oz fresh coriander, chopped

1 preserved lemon, chopped

1 tbsp walnuts, chopped

seeds from 1 pomegranate

24 jalapeño chillies, halved and deseeded

2 avocados, peeled, stoned and sliced

juice of 1 lemon

salt and pepper (optional)

Method

1 To make tabbouleh, cook the quinoa according to the packet instructions. Drain and refresh under cold water, then drain again. Place in a large bowl.

2 Add the parsley, mint, coriander, preserved lemon, walnuts and pomegranate seeds and mix thoroughly. Season to taste with salt and pepper, if using.

3 Spoon the tabbouleh into the jalapeños. Top each one with a couple of slices of avocado, then squeeze over the lemon juice to serve.

★ Variations

If you want to reduce the strength of the jalapeños, lightly blanch them first. For a different topping, try a tbsp of gluten-free hummus, sprinkled with toasted sunflower seeds and smoked paprika. You can also vary the choice of herbs – chives, fennel and dill could also be used.

SPICY FALAFELS

Serves: 4   **Prep: 25 mins**   **Cook: 10-15 mins**

Ingredients

400 g/14 oz canned chickpeas, drained and rinsed

1 small red onion, chopped

2 garlic cloves, crushed

2 tsp ground coriander

1½ tsp ground cumin

1 tsp ground star anise

1 fresh red chilli, chopped

1 egg white

½ tsp gluten-free baking powder

gram flour, for shaping

sunflower oil, for deep-frying

salt and pepper (optional)

Salad

1 large orange

2 tbsp extra virgin olive oil

55 g/2 oz rocket leaves

salt and pepper (optional)

Method

1 Place the chickpeas, onion, garlic, coriander, cumin, anise, chilli, egg white and salt and pepper, if using, in a blender or food processor and process to a firm, but still textured, paste. Stir in the baking powder.

2 Use a little gram flour on your hands to shape the mixture into 12 small balls.

3 To make the salad, cut all the peel and white pith from the orange and lift out the segments, catching the juice. Whisk the orange juice with the olive oil and season to taste, if using salt and pepper. Lightly toss the orange segments and rocket with the dressing.

4 Heat a 2.5 cm/1 inch depth of oil in a large pan to 180°C/350°F, or until a cube of bread browns in 30 seconds. Fry the falafels for about 2 minutes, until golden brown.

5 Drain the falafels on kitchen paper and serve with the salad.

INDIAN SPICED SLAW

Serves: 4

Prep: 20 mins plus cooling

Cook: 5 mins

Ingredients

175 g/6 oz red cabbage, shredded

40 g/1½ oz kale, shredded

1 red apple, cored and coarsely grated

1 large carrot, coarsely grated

Topping

2 tbsp pumpkin seeds

2 tbsp sunflower seeds

2 tbsp flaked almonds

½ tsp gluten-free garam masala

¼ tsp ground turmeric

1 tbsp sunflower oil

Dressing

150 g/5½ oz natural yogurt

1 tsp gluten-free garam masala

¼ tsp ground turmeric

salt and pepper (optional)

Method

1 To make the topping, preheat a frying pan over a medium heat. Put the pumpkin seeds, sunflower seeds, almonds, garam masala and turmeric in the hot pan and pour on the oil. Cook for 3–4 minutes, stirring often, until the almonds are golden-brown. Leave to cool.

2 To make the dressing, put the yogurt, garam masala and turmeric in a large bowl, then season to taste with salt and pepper, if using, and stir well.

3 Add the cabbage, kale, apple and carrot to the bowl and toss gently together. Divide the salad between four bowls, sprinkle on the topping and serve.

HOT & SOUR COURGETTES

Serves: 4　　**Prep: 15–20 mins**　　**Cook: 5 mins**
　　　　　　　　plus standing

Ingredients

2 large courgettes, thinly sliced

1 tsp salt

2 tbsp groundnut oil

1 tsp Sichuan peppercorns, crushed

½–1 red chilli, deseeded and sliced into thin strips

1 large garlic clove, thinly sliced

½ tsp finely chopped fresh ginger

1 tbsp rice vinegar

1 tbsp gluten-free tamari

2 tsp sugar

1 spring onion, green part included, thinly sliced

a few drops of sesame oil and 1 tsp sesame seeds, to garnish

Method

1 Put the courgette slices in a large colander and toss with the salt. Cover with a plate and put a weight on top. Leave to drain for 20 minutes. Rinse off the salt and spread out the slices on kitchen paper to dry.

2 Preheat a wok over a high heat and add the groundnut oil. Add the Sichuan peppercorns, chilli, garlic and ginger. Fry for about 20 seconds until the garlic is just beginning to colour.

3 Add the courgette slices and toss in the oil. Add the rice vinegar, tamari and sugar, and stir-fry for 2 minutes. Add the spring onion and fry for 30 seconds. Garnish with the sesame oil and seeds and serve immediately.

CHILLI & AMARANTH CORNBREAD

Serves: 1 loaf   **Prep: 20 mins**   **Cook: 55 mins**

Ingredients

10 g/¼ oz butter, for greasing

2–3 fresh red chillies

90 g/3¼ oz amaranth flour

100 g/3½ oz gluten-free white flour mixture

115 g/4 oz coarse polenta (cornmeal)

1 tbsp gluten-free baking powder

1 tsp gluten-free bicarbonate of soda

1½ tsp salt

50 g/1¾ oz sugar

125 g/4½ oz Cheddar cheese, roughly grated

3 eggs

225 ml/8 fl oz buttermilk

70 g/2½ oz butter, melted and slightly cooled

60 g/2¼ oz fresh or frozen sweetcorn kernels, thawed if frozen

Method

1 Preheat the oven to 200°C/400°F/Gas Mark 6. Preheat the grill. Grease a 900 g/2 lb loaf tin.

2 Place the chillies under the preheated grill and cook, turning occasionally, for 5–7 minutes, until blackened all over. Remove the skins and seeds and finely chop the flesh.

3 Sift together the amaranth flour, white flour mixture, polenta, baking powder, bicarbonate of soda and salt into a large bowl. Stir in the sugar and cheese.

4 Whisk the eggs with the buttermilk and melted butter until well blended.

5 Make a well in the centre of the flour mixture and pour in the egg mixture. Mix together with a fork, gradually drawing in the dry ingredients from the side.

6 Stir in the chillies and sweetcorn and spoon the batter into the prepared tin, levelling the surface. Bake in the preheated oven for 40–45 minutes, until a skewer inserted into the centre comes out clean.

7 Leave to cool in the tin for 10 minutes, then turn out onto a wire rack and leave to cool completely.

TOMATO FOCACCIA

Makes: 1 loaf

Prep: 25 mins
plus rising and cooling

Cook: 35 mins

Ingredients

3 tbsp olive oil, plus extra
for brushing

200 g/7 oz buckwheat flour

200 g/7 oz potato flour

200 g/7 oz rice flour

2 tsp xanthan gum

7 g/⅓ oz sachet gluten-free
fast-action yeast

1½ tsp salt

½ tsp black onion seeds

40 g/1½ oz sun-dried
tomatoes, soaked, drained
and chopped

600 ml/1 pint tepid water

1 small egg, beaten

2 garlic cloves,
cut into slivers

few sprigs fresh oregano

Method

1 Brush a 33 x 23-cm/13 x 9-inch baking sheet with oil. Mix the flours, xanthan gum, yeast, salt and onion seeds in a bowl and stir in the tomatoes.

2 Make a well in the centre and stir in the water, egg and 1 tablespoon of oil to make a very soft dough. Beat the dough hard using a wooden spoon for 4–5 minutes, then spoon into the tin, spreading evenly with a palette knife.

3 Cover with oiled cling film and leave in a warm place for about 1 hour, or until doubled in size. Preheat the oven to 220°C/425°F/Gas Mark 7.

4 Press pieces of garlic and oregano into the dough at intervals. Drizzle with the remaining oil, then bake in the oven for 25–30 minutes, or until firm and golden brown. Turn out and cool on a wire rack.

SUMMER POTATO SALAD

Serves: 4

Prep: 5–10 mins

Cook: 25–30 mins, plus cooling

Ingredients

500 g/1 lb 2 oz new potatoes, with skin on

5 spring onions

1 handful fresh mint leaves

1 handful fresh parsley

Dressing

4 tbsp extra virgin rapeseed oil

1 tbsp white wine vinegar

1 tsp caster sugar

1 tsp gluten-free French mustard

salt and pepper (optional)

Method

1 Put the potatoes in a saucepan, cover with water, add a little salt, if using, and place over a medium–high heat. Bring to the boil and simmer for about 20 minutes, or until the potatoes are tender.

2 While the potatoes are cooking, slice the spring onions, retaining most of the green parts, and finely chop the mint and parsley. In a bowl, mix together the oil, vinegar, sugar, mustard and seasoning, if using.

3 Drain the potatoes and return them in the pan to the hot hob (switched off) for 1 minute to evaporate any remaining moisture.

4 While the potatoes are still hot, tip them into a bowl and roughly chop them. Add the spring onions, herbs and dressing and stir to mix thoroughly. Cover and leave for 1 hour before serving for the potatoes to absorb the oil and flavourings.

BUCKWHEAT FLATBREADS

Makes: 4

Prep: 20 mins

Cook: 10 mins

Ingredients

200 g/7 oz buckwheat flour

100 g/3½ oz rice flour

1 tsp salt

1 tsp gluten-free baking powder

½ tsp ground cumin

2 tbsp chopped fresh coriander

200 ml/7 fl oz water

2 tbsp olive oil

10 g/¼ oz buckwheat flour, for dusting

Method

1 Sift together the buckwheat flour, rice flour, salt, baking powder and cumin into a large bowl and make a well in the centre.

2 Add the coriander, water and oil and stir into the dry ingredients to make a soft dough.

3 Divide the dough into four pieces and shape each piece into a smooth ball. Roll out each ball on a lightly floured surface to a 20 cm/ 8 inch round.

4 Preheat a griddle pan or barbecue to very hot. Add the flatbreads and cook for about 1 minute on each side, or until firm and golden brown. Serve warm.

SWEET POTATO CHIPS

Serves: 4   **Prep: 10 mins**   **Cook: 25 mins**

Ingredients

1 litre/1¾ pints vegetable oil

60 g/2¼ oz gluten-free plain flour

1 tsp salt

225 ml/8 fl oz water, plus extra if needed

900 g/2 lb orange-fleshed sweet potatoes, peeled and cut into 5-mm/¼-inch sticks

sea salt (optional)

Method

1 Place the oil in a large, heavy-based saucepan or a deep-fryer. If using a saucepan, attach a deep-frying thermometer. Heat the oil to 180–190°C/350–375°F, or until a cube of bread browns in 30 seconds.

2 Meanwhile, combine the flour and salt in a medium-sized bowl. Whisk in the water until well combined. The batter should be the consistency of a very thin pancake batter. If it is too thick, add more water, 1 tablespoon at a time. If it is too thin, add more flour, 1 tablespoon at a time.

3 Add a handful of the sweet potatoes to the batter and stir to coat. Remove from the batter using tongs, allowing the excess to drip back into the bowl. Transfer the battered potatoes to the hot oil and cook for 3–4 minutes, until golden brown and crisp. Remove using tongs and drain on a plate lined with kitchen paper. Continue cooking in batches until all of the potatoes are cooked. Season generously with sea salt, if using, and serve immediately.

SNACKS & LIGHT BITES

LUNCHES

ASIAN SALAD WITH COCONUT RICE

Serves: 6   **Prep: 20 mins**   **Cook: 25-30 mins**

Ingredients

1 x 160 ml/5½ fl oz can coconut cream

450 ml/15 fl oz water

250 g/9 oz jasmine rice, rinsed

3 kaffir lime leaves

pinch of salt

½ large red cabbage, shredded

60 g/2¼ oz peanuts, roughly chopped

zest and juice of 1 lime

30 g/1 oz fresh coriander, roughly chopped

30 g/1 oz fresh mint, roughly chopped

1 spring onion, finely sliced

2 tbsp sesame oil

1 tbsp sesame seeds, toasted

pepper (optional)

Method

1 Pour the coconut cream and water into a medium-sized pan and bring to the boil. Add the rice, lime leaves and salt. Reduce the heat, cover and cook on a low heat for 15-20 minute until most of the liquid has been absorbed. Remove from the heat and cover the pan for 5 minutes.

2 Stir the shredded cabbage through the rice along with half of the peanuts, the lime zest and half of the herbs. Season with pepper to taste, if using.

3 Spoon the rice mixture onto a serving plate and top with the spring onion, the remaining herbs and the peanuts. Spritz with lime juice and serve with a drizzle of sesame oil and a sprinkling of sesame seeds.

★ **Variation**

Try switching the coconut rice with vermicelli noodles for a summery version of this salad.

SWEET POTATO NOODLES WITH TAHINI & TAMARIND

Serves: 4   **Prep: 15 mins**   **Cook: 10 mins**

Ingredients

2 sweet potatoes
(about 500 g/1 lb 2 oz)

2 pak choi

30 g/1 oz fresh coriander,
roughly chopped

5 spring onions,
roughly chopped

1 red chilli, deseeded
and finely sliced

40 g/1½ oz cashew nuts,
toasted

Dressing

2 garlic cloves, peeled
and crushed

pinch of salt

¼ tsp caster sugar

1 tbsp tamarind paste

1 tbsp gluten-free tahini

5 tbsp boiling water

Method

1 Prepare the noodles by peeling and spiralizing the sweet potatoes. Set the spiralized potatoes aside for 1–2 minutes.

2 Boil a large pan of water. Blanch the pak choi and sweet potato noodles for 3 minutes, until both are just cooked but still have a healthy bite. Drain the noodles and immediately transfer them to a large bowl.

3 To make the dressing, put the garlic, salt, sugar, tamarind paste, tahini and water into a jar. Cover with a lid and shake well.

4 Combine the sweet potato noodles and pak choi with the dressing, making sure the noodles are well coated. Transfer the noodles to a platter and gently combine them with the spring onion, red chilli and cashew nuts. Serve immediately.

BLACK BEAN & QUINOA BURRITOS

Makes: 8　　　　　**Prep: 30 mins**　　　　　**Cook: 20 mins**

Ingredients

60 g/2¼ oz red quinoa, rinsed

150 ml/5 fl oz water

2 tbsp vegetable oil

1 red onion, diced

1 fresh green chilli, deseeded and diced

1 small red pepper, deseeded and diced

400 g/14 oz canned black beans, drained and rinsed

juice of 1 lime

4 tbsp chopped fresh coriander

2 tomatoes

8 gluten-free corn tortillas, warmed

125 g/4½ oz Cheddar cheese, roughly grated

85 g/3 oz shredded cos lettuce

salt and pepper (optional)

Method

1 Put the quinoa into a saucepan with the water. Bring to the boil, then cover and simmer over a very low heat for 15 minutes. Remove from the heat, but leave the pan covered for a further 5 minutes to allow the grains to swell. Fluff up with a fork and set aside.

2 Heat the oil in a frying pan. Fry half the onion, half the chilli and the red pepper until soft. Add the beans, quinoa and half the lime juice and coriander. Fry for a few minutes, then season to taste with salt and pepper, if using.

3 Halve the tomatoes and scoop out the seeds. Add the seeds to the bean mixture. Dice the tomato flesh and place in a bowl with the remaining coriander, onion, chilli and lime juice and salt to taste, if using. Stir.

4 Place 5 tablespoons of the bean mixture on top of each tortilla. Sprinkle with the tomato salsa, cheese and lettuce. Fold the end and sides over the filling, roll up and serve immediately.

LUNCHES

SPICY TOMATO, TAMARIND & GINGER SOUP

Serves: 4 **Prep: 15 mins** **Cook: 35 mins**

Ingredients

60 g/2¼ oz butter

1 small onion, diced

2-cm/¾-inch piece fresh ginger, finely chopped

1 tsp ground turmeric

2 tsp cumin seeds, crushed

¼ tsp salt

½ tsp pepper

400 g/14 oz canned chopped tomatoes

2 tsp tamarind paste

70 g/2½ oz red quinoa, rinsed

225 ml/8 fl oz gluten-free vegetable stock

4 tbsp chopped fresh coriander

Method

1 Heat half the butter in a large saucepan. Add the onion and fry over a low–medium heat for 5 minutes, until translucent.

2 Add the ginger, turmeric, ½ teaspoon of the cumin seeds, the salt and pepper. Cook for a further minute.

3 Stir in the tomatoes, tamarind paste, quinoa and stock. Bring to the boil, then reduce the heat, cover and simmer for 25 minutes, stirring occasionally.

4 Remove from the heat and stir in the coriander Leave to stand, covered, for 10 minutes.

5 Heat the remaining butter in a small frying pan over a medium–high heat. Add the remaining cumin seeds and sizzle for a few seconds. Swirl into the soup and serve immediately.

FARRO & BORLOTTI BEAN SOUP

Serves: 4–6   **Prep: 15 mins**   **Cook: 55 mins**

Ingredients

115 g/4 oz quick-cook farro, rinsed

1 tbsp olive oil

1 tbsp finely chopped fresh rosemary

100 g/3½ oz pancetta, diced

1 onion, diced

2 celery sticks, diced

1 small red pepper, deseeded and diced

850 ml/1½ pints gluten-free chicken stock

100 g/3½ oz canned, borlotti beans, rinsed and drained

4–6 slices gluten-free ciabatta bread, toasted

salt and pepper (optional)

3 tbsp extra virgin olive oil for drizzling

1 tbsp chopped fresh flat-leaf parsley, to garnish

Method

1 Put the farro into a saucepan with water to cover. Add ½ teaspoon of salt, and bring to the boil. Reduce the heat and simmer for 10–12 minutes, until tender but still chewy. Drain, reserving the liquid.

2 Meanwhile, heat the olive oil with the rosemary in a large saucepan. Add the pancetta and onion and fry gently for 5 minutes, until the onion is translucent.

3 Add the celery and red pepper. Season to taste with salt and pepper, if using, and cook for a further 5 minutes. Pour in the stock, cover and simmer for 15 minutes, until the vegetables are tender.

4 Add the cooked farro and the beans. Cook for 15 minutes, uncovered, until thick and soupy. Add some of the reserved farro cooking liquid if the mixture becomes too thick.

5 Place a slice of bread in the base of four to six bowls. Ladle over the soup. Drizzle with extra virgin olive oil, sprinkle with parsley and serve.

CHICKPEA FRITTERS

Serves: 4　　**Prep: 20 mins**　　**Cook: 20 mins**

Ingredients

125 g/4½ oz gluten-free self-raising flour

1 egg, beaten

175 ml/6 fl oz milk

140 g/5 oz spring onions, thinly sliced

400 g/14 oz canned chickpeas, rinsed and drained

4 tbsp chopped fresh coriander

sunflower oil, for frying

salt and pepper (optional)

coriander sprigs, to garnish

Method

1 Sift the flour into a bowl and make a well in the centre. Add the egg and milk and stir into the flour, then whisk to make a smooth batter.

2 Stir in the onions, chickpeas and coriander, then season well with salt and pepper, if using.

3 Heat the oil in a large, heavy-based frying pan and add tablespoonfuls of the batter. Fry in batches for 4–5 minutes, turning once, until golden brown.

4 Serve the fritters stacked on warmed serving plates, garnished with coriander sprigs.

ROASTED PEPPER SALAD

Serves: 4

Prep: 10-15 mins
plus chilling

Cook: 40 mins

Ingredients

2 red peppers, halved
and deseeded

2 yellow peppers, halved
and deseeded

1 red onion,
roughly chopped

2 garlic cloves,
finely chopped

6 tbsp olive oil

100 g/3½ oz mini
mozzarella cheese pearls,
drained

2 tbsp roughly torn
fresh basil

2 tbsp balsamic vinegar

salt and pepper (optional)

Method

1 Preheat the oven to 190°C/375°F/Gas Mark 5. Put the peppers cut side up in a shallow roasting tin. Scatter over the onion and garlic, season well with salt and pepper, if using, and drizzle over 3 tablespoons of the olive oil. Roast for 40 minutes, or until the peppers are tender. Leave to cool.

2 Arrange the cold peppers in a serving dish and pour over any juices left in the roasting tin. Scatter over the mozzarella and basil.

3 To make the dressing, whisk together the remaining olive oil and the balsamic vinegar, then drizzle over the peppers. Cover and leave to marinate in the refrigerator for at least 2 hours before serving.

LUNCHES

PROTEIN RICE BOWL

Serves: 2

Prep: 25 mins

Cook: 30 mins

Ingredients

150 g/5½ oz brown rice

2 large eggs

70 g/2½ oz spinach

4 spring onions, finely chopped

1 red chilli, deseeded and finely sliced

½ ripe avocado, sliced

2 tbsp roasted peanuts

Vinaigrette

2 tbsp olive oil

1 tsp gluten-free Dijon mustard

1 tbsp cider vinegar

juice of ½ lemon

Method

1 Place the rice in a large saucepan and cover with twice the volume of water. Bring to the boil and simmer for 25 minutes, or until the rice is tender and the liquid has nearly all disappeared. Continue to simmer for a further few minutes if some liquid remains.

2 Meanwhile, cook your eggs. Bring a small saucepan of water to the boil. Carefully add the eggs to the pan and boil for 7 minutes – the whites will be cooked and the yolks should still be very slightly soft. Drain and pour cold water over the eggs to stop them cooking. When cool enough to handle, tap them on the work surface to crack the shells and peel them. Cut the eggs into quarters.

3 Stir the spinach, half of the spring onions and a little red chilli into the cooked rice.

4 To make the vinaigrette, whisk the olive oil, Dijon mustard, cider vinegar and lemon juice together. Pour the dressing over the warm rice and mix to combine.

5 Divide the rice between two bowls and top each with the remaining spring onions, avocado, remaining red chilli, peanuts and egg quarters.

SQUASH, PINE NUTS & GOAT'S CHEESE PIZZA

Serves: 6

Prep: 30 mins
plus resting

Cook: 50–55 mins

Ingredients

1 egg white

3 tbsp vegetable oil

½ tsp vinegar

1 tbsp caster sugar

½ tsp salt

200 ml/7 fl oz water

250 g/9 oz gluten-free white bread flour

1 tsp quick gluten-free yeast

Pizza topping

½ large squash, peeled, deseeded and cut into crescents

3 fresh rosemary sprigs, roughly chopped

1 tbsp olive oil

125 ml/4 fl oz soured cream

100 g/3½ oz goat's cheese, cut into rounds

50 g/1¾ oz pine nuts

pepper (optional)

Method

1 Line a large oven tray with baking paper.

2 Put the egg white, half of the vegetable oil, the vinegar, sugar, salt and water into a bowl and whisk well. Add the flour and yeast, mixing to a smooth, thick batter.

3 Pour the remaining oil over the batter and turn with a spoon until you have a soft dough. Spoon the dough onto the baking paper and mould into a rough 25 cm/10 inch circle. Leave to rest in a dry place for 30 minutes.

4 Meanwhile, preheat the oven to 200°C/400°F/Gas Mark 6. Place the squash crescents on a large baking tray and drizzle over the olive oil and half of the rosemary.

5 Roast the crescents for 20 minutes, turning them halfway through, until they are beginning to turn golden. Remove from the oven and increase the temperature to 220°C/425°F/Gas Mark 7.

6 Spread the soured cream over the pizza base and top with the squash, goat's cheese, pine nuts and the remaining rosemary. Season with pepper to taste, if using.

7 Bake for 30–35 minutes, until the base has puffed up and the cheese is golden and bubbling. Serve immediately.

RED QUINOA & CHICKPEA SALAD

Serves: 4   **Prep: 10–15 mins**   **Cook: 15–20 mins**

Ingredients

50 g/1¾ red quinoa

1 red chilli, deseeded and finely chopped

8 spring onions, chopped

3 tbsp finely chopped fresh mint

2 tbsp olive oil

2 tbsp fresh lemon juice

30 g/1 oz chickpea (gram) flour

1 tsp ground cumin

½ tsp paprika

1 tbsp vegetable oil

150 g/5½ oz canned chickpeas, drained and rinsed

Method

1 Place the quinoa in a medium saucepan and then cover with boiling water. Place over a low heat and simmer for 10 minutes, or until just cooked. Drain and refresh with cold water, drain again. Transfer to a large bowl and toss together with the red chilli, spring onion and mint to mix thoroughly.

2 Combine the olive oil and lemon juice in a small bowl using a fork.

3 Sift the chickpea flour, cumin and paprika together into a wide, deep bowl. Place the vegetable oil in a medium frying pan over a medium heat. Roll the chickpeas in the spiced flour then fry gently in the pan, stirring frequently for 2–3 minutes, allowing the chickpeas to brown in patches.

4 Stir the warm chickpeas into the quinoa mixture and quickly stir in the lemon-oil dressing. Serve warm or chilled.

QUINOA & WALNUT TABBOULEH

Serves: 4　　　**Prep: 20 mins**　　　**Cook: 20 mins,**
plus standing

Ingredients

100 g/3½ oz white quinoa, rinsed

250 ml/9 fl oz water

1 courgette, coarsely grated

2 large spring onions, thinly sliced diagonally

handful of fresh mint leaves, chopped

handful of fresh flat-leaf parsley leaves, chopped

8 walnut halves, chopped

Dressing

3 tbsp extra virgin olive oil

1 tbsp lemon juice

1 tsp gluten-free Dijon mustard

1 garlic clove, crushed

pepper (optional)

Method

1 Put the quinoa into a saucepan with the water. Bring to the boil, then cover and simmer over a very low heat for 15 minutes. Remove from the heat, but leave the pan covered for a further 5 minutes to allow the grains to swell. Fluff up with a fork.

2 Transfer the cooked quinoa to a bowl and add the courgette, spring onions, mint and parsley.

3 Mix together the ingredients for the dressing, then pour over the quinoa mixture. Stir gently until just combined.

4 Transfer to two plates and sprinkle with the walnuts. Serve at room temperature.

SOUTH INDIAN LENTIL BROTH

Serves: 4   **Prep: 10 mins**   **Cook: 30–35 mins**

Ingredients

100 g/3½ oz pigeon peas (tuvaar dal)

600 ml/1 pint cold water

1 tsp ground turmeric

2 tbsp vegetable or groundnut oil

1 tsp black mustard seeds

6–8 fresh curry leaves

1 tsp cumin seeds

1 fresh green chilli, chopped

1 tsp tamarind paste

1 tsp salt

Method

1 Rinse the pigeon peas under cold running water and place in a saucepan with the water, turmeric and 1 tablespoon of the oil. Cover and simmer for 25–30 minutes, or until cooked and tender.

2 Heat the remaining oil in a frying pan over a medium heat. Add the mustard seeds, curry leaves, cumin seeds, chilli and tamarind paste. When the seeds start to pop, remove the pan from the heat and add to the pigeon pea mixture with the salt.

3 Return the broth to the heat for 2–3 minutes. Ladle into small serving bowls and serve immediately.

BASIL GNOCCHI

Serves: 4   **Prep: 35 mins**   **Cook: 40–50 mins**

Ingredients

500 g/1 lb 2 oz floury
potatoes (e.g. Maris Piper)

osp finely chopped basil

½ tsp ground nutmeg

100 g/3½ oz gluten-free
ain white flour blend, plus
extra for dusting

1 small egg, beaten

4 plum tomatoes, halved

1 red onion, halved

2 garlic cloves

oil, for brushing

t and pepper (optional)

basil leaves, to garnish

Method

1 Peel the potatoes and cut into chunks. Cook in lightly salted, boiling water for 15–20 minutes or until tender. Drain thoroughly.

2 Press the potatoes through a potato ricer or coarse sieve. Add the chopped basil and season well with nutmeg and salt and pepper, if using. Lightly stir in the flour and add enough egg to make a fairly soft, but not sticky, dough.

3 Divide the dough into four and roll each piece to a sausage about 20 cm/8 inch long, 2.5 cm/1 inch wide. Cut each into 8–9 slices. Roll each into a ball and press over a floured fork with your thumb, making ridges on one side and an indentation on the other.

4 Preheat a grill to hot. Place the tomatoes and onion cut side down onto a baking sheet with the garlic cloves and brush with oil. Grill for 8–10 minutes until the skins are charred. Remove the skins and roughly chop.

5 Bring a large pan of water to the boil, and cook the gnocchi in batches for 4–6 minutes, or until they rise to the surface. Lift out with a slotted spoon.

6 Serve the gnocchi hot, with the tomato sauce spooned over and garnish with basil leaves.

LUNCHES

SWEET ROOTS BOWL

Serves: 4 **Prep: 12 mins** **Cook: 35–40 mins**

Ingredients

2 sweet potatoes,
cut into chunks

2 beetroot,
cut into chunks

2 red onions,
cut into wedges

2 tbsp olive oil

2 tsp cumin seeds

75 g/2¾ oz brown rice

4 tbsp gluten-free tahini

juice of 1 lemon

½ tsp pepper

½ tsp honey

200 g/7 oz kale, shredded

2 tbsp flaked almonds,
toasted

Method

1 Preheat the oven to 200°C/400°F/Gas Mark 6.

2 Place the sweet potatoes, beetroot and onions in a bowl with the oil and cumin seeds and toss together to coat with the oil.

3 Tip into a roasting tin and roast in the preheated oven for 35–40 minutes, until tender.

4 Meanwhile, cook the rice according to the packet instructions.

5 Whisk together the tahini, lemon juice, pepper and honey.

6 Stir the kale into the root vegetables 10 minutes before the end of the roasting time.

7 Drain the rice and divide between four warmed bowls.

8 Toss the vegetables with the dressing and serve on top of the rice, sprinkled with the toasted almonds.

COURGETTE QUICHE

Serves: 4

Prep: 25–30 mins
plus chilling & cooling

Cook: 55 mins–1 hour

Ingredients

200 g/7 oz gluten-free plain white flour blend

100 g/3½ oz butter

3 tbsp snipped fresh chives

4–5 tbsp cold water

a pinch of salt

Filling

2 tbsp olive oil

1 small red onion, cut into wedges

2 courgettes, cut into 2-cm/¾-inch chunks

8 cherry tomatoes, halved

1 large egg, beaten

175 ml/6 fl oz milk

salt and pepper (optional)

Method

1 For the pastry, place the flour, butter and chives with the salt in a food processor and process to fine crumbs. Mix in just enough water to bind the mixture to a firm dough.

2 Roll out on a lightly floured surface to line a 19-cm/7½-inch diameter, 5-cm/2¾-inch deep, loose-based flan tin. Prick the base with a fork and chill in the refrigerator for 10 minutes.

3 Preheat the oven to 200°C/400°C/Gas Mark 6 and preheat a baking sheet. Line the pastry case with baking paper and dried beans and bake blind in the preheated oven for 10 minutes. Remove the paper and beans and bake for a further 5 minutes. Reduce the oven temperature to 190°C/375°F/Gas Mark 5.

4 For the filling, heat the oil and fry the onion and courgettes, stirring often, for 4–5 minutes, or until softened and lightly browned. Tip into the pastry case with the tomatoes.

5 Beat the egg with the milk and season well, if using salt and pepper. Pour into the pastry case. Bake in the preheated oven for 35–40 minutes, or until golden brown and set. Cool for 10 minutes before turning out. Serve the quiche warm or cold.

GOLDEN PILAF

Serves: 4   **Prep: 15 mins**   **Cook: 30–35mins**

Ingredients

450 ml/16 fl oz gluten-free vegetable or chicken stock

200 g/7 oz toasted buckwheat

3 tbsp olive oil

1 medium onion, sliced

2 garlic cloves, thinly sliced

2-cm/¾-inch piece fresh ginger, thinly sliced

½ tsp ground turmeric

½ tsp ground cinnamon

4 tbsp orange juice

85 g/3 oz sultanas

2 medium carrots, coarsely grated

55 g/2 oz pine nuts, toasted

salt and pepper (optional)

shreds of orange zest and coriander, to garnish

Method

1 Bring the stock to the boil and add the buckwheat. Simmer for 5–6 minutes until most of the liquid is absorbed, and then add 1 tablespoon of the oil, cover and leave on a low heat for 10 minutes, until tender.

2 Heat the remaining oil and fry the onion on a medium heat for 5–6 minutes, stirring occasionally, until soft and golden brown.

3 Add the garlic and ginger and stir for 1 minute, then stir in the turmeric, cinnamon, orange juice and sultanas and cook for 1 minute.

4 Add the carrots, cooked buckwheat and pine nuts, stirring until evenly heated. Season to taste with salt and pepper, if using.

5 Pile the pilaf onto a warm serving plate and scatter over the orange zest and coriander. Serve either on its own or as an accompaniment to grilled or roasted meats.

GINGERED CARROT & POMEGRANATE SALAD

Serves: 4   **Prep: 10–15 mins**   **Cook: none**

Ingredients

350 g/12 oz carrots,
finely grated

5-cm/2-inch piece fresh
ginger, peeled and
finely grated

1 small pomegranate,
quartered

50 g/1¾ oz ready-to-eat
sprouting seeds, such as
alfalfa and radish sprouts

Topping

3 tbsp light olive oil

3 tsp red wine vinegar

3 tsp pomegranate
molasses

salt and pepper (optional)

Method

1 Put the carrots and ginger in a salad bowl. Flex the pomegranate pieces to pop out the seeds, prising any stubborn ones out with the tip of a small knife, and add to the bowl.

2 To make the dressing, put the oil, vinegar and pomegranate molasses in a jam jar, season with salt and pepper, if using, screw on the lid and shake well. Drizzle over the salad and toss gently together. Cover and leave to marinate in the refrigerator for 30 minutes.

3 Sprinkle the sprouting seeds over the salad and serve.

CHICKEN & VEGETABLE SOUP

Serves: 4   **Prep: 15–20 mins**   **Cook: 1 hour 20 mins**

Ingredients

1 onion, finely chopped

1 garlic clove, finely chopped

115 g/4 oz white cabbage, shredded

2 carrots, finely chopped

4 potatoes, diced

1 green pepper, cored, deseeded and diced

400 g/14 oz canned chopped tomatoes

1.3 litres/2¼ pints gluten-free chicken stock

175 g/6 oz cooked chicken, diced

salt and pepper (optional)

2 tbsp chopped fresh flat-leaf parsley, to garnish

Method

1 Put all the ingredients, except the chicken and parsley, in a large saucepan and bring to the boil. Simmer for 1 hour, or until the vegetables are tender.

2 Add the chicken and simmer for a further 10 minutes, or until hot.

3 Ladle the soup into warmed bowls and serve immediately, garnished with parsley.

MELON, PARMA HAM & PECORINO SALAD

Serves: 4 **Prep: 10–15 mins** **Cook: none**

Ingredients

400 g/14 oz watermelon flesh, thinly sliced

400 g/14 oz honeydew melon flesh, thinly sliced

400 g/14 oz cantaloupe melon flesh, thinly sliced

140 g/5 oz sliced Parma ham

25 g/1 oz fresh pecorino cheese shavings

25 g/1 oz fresh basil

Dressing

4 tbsp light olive oil

1 tbsp aged sherry vinegar

salt and pepper (optional)

Method

1 Arrange the watermelon, honeydew melon and cantaloupe melon slices on a large serving platter. Tear any large Parma ham slices in half, then fold them all over and around the melon.

2 To make the dressing, put the olive oil and sherry vinegar in a jam jar, season well with salt and pepper, if using, screw on the lid and shake well. Drizzle over the melon and Parma ham.

3 Sprinkle on the pecorino and basil. Serve immediately.

LUNCHES

PANCETTA, SPINACH & CHICKEN SALAD

Serves: 4　　　　**Prep: 30 mins**　　　　**Cook: 40 mins**

Ingredients

5 skinless chicken thighs (about 450 g/1 lb), halved

1 tsp olive oil, for brushing

2–3 fresh thyme sprigs

300 g/10½ oz gluten-free pasta twirls

150 g/5½ oz baby spinach, washed

100 g/3½ oz pancetta

½ red onion, very finely sliced

salt and pepper (optional)

2 tbsp snipped fresh chives, to serve

Dressing

2 tbsp olive oil

1 garlic clove, crushed

1 tbsp gluten-free Dijon mustard

2 tbsp cider vinegar

salt and pepper (optional)

Method

1 Preheat the oven to 200°C/400°F/Gas Mark 6.

2 On a roasting tray, place the chicken thighs and brush each with a little olive oil. Scatter over the thyme and season with salt and pepper, if using.

3 Place in the centre of the oven and cook for 20 minutes, until the chicken is tender and the juices run clear when a skewer is inserted into the thickest part of the meat. Remove from the oven and allow the chicken to cool.

4 Bring a large pan of water to the boil and add the pasta twirls. Simmer for 7–8 minutes, until the pasta is al dente. Drain, return to the pan and immediately stir the baby spinach through the pasta. The spinach will wilt in the residual heat.

5 Heat a medium-sized frying pan over a high heat and fry the pancetta until it is golden and crisp. Set aside.

6 Once the chicken is cool enough to handle, tear into strips. Arrange the chicken, pancetta, pasta, spinach and red onion on a large platter.

7 For the dressing, put the olive oil, garlic, mustard and cider vinegar in a jar. Add seasoning, if using. Shake until the dressing is emulsified and smooth and spoon over the salad leaves. Serve immediately, scattered with chives.

SWEET & SPICY MEATBALLS

Serves: 4

Prep: 20 mins
plus chilling

Cook: 45–50 mins

Ingredients

1 tbsp olive oil

2 spring onions, finely chopped

400 g/14 oz beef mince

5½ tsp chilli flakes

50 g/1¾ oz dried apricots, finely chopped

1 egg

2 tbsp gluten-free plain flour

salt and pepper (optional)

1 tbsp chopped fresh flat-leaf parsley, to garnish

steamed white rice, to serve

Tomato sauce

1 tbsp olive oil

½ onion, roughly chopped

3 garlic cloves, sliced

1 tsp ground cumin

1 tbsp gluten-free tomato purée

1 x 400 g/14 oz can chopped tomatoes

salt and pepper (optional)

Method

1. Heat 1 tablespoon of the olive oil in a pan over a medium heat. Add the onion and cook for 4– minutes. Set the pan aside to cool.

2. To make the meatballs, put the mince, chilli flakes, apricots and spring onions in a large bowl. Lightly whisk the egg and add to the mixture. Add seasoning, if using, and combine.

3. Divide the mixture into 12 equal-sized balls. Sprinkle the flour onto a plate and roll the meatballs in the flour. Chill for 10 minutes.

4. Heat the remaining oil in a frying pan, add the meatballs and cook for 5 minutes over a medium–high heat without moving them. Turn them over and cook for another 5 minutes before removing them and setting them aside.

5. To make the tomato sauce, return the softened onion to the pan with the garlic and cumin. Cook over a medium–low heat for 1–2 minutes before adding the tomato purée and tomatoes Season with salt and pepper, if using.

6. Cook the sauce for 2–3 minutes before returning the meatballs to the pan. Cover and gently cook for 20 minutes, or until the meatballs are cooked through. Garnish the meatballs with chopped parsley and serve with white rice.

GINGERED STEAK LETTUCE BOATS

Serves: 4

Prep: 15 mins
plus marinating

Cook: 5 mins

Ingredients

2 tbsp gluten-free
soy sauce

2 tbsp honey

1 tsp gluten-free smooth
mustard

2 garlic cloves, crushed

30 g/1 oz fresh ginger,
peeled and finely diced

400 g/14 oz rump steak,
cut into strips

8 spring onions, shredded

1 carrot, grated

¼ cucumber, cut into
julienne strips

25 g/1 oz mangetout,
cut into julienne strips

4 Little Gem lettuces,
leaves separated

small handful of fresh
coriander sprigs (optional)

2 tbsp sesame seeds,
toasted (optional)

Method

1 Mix the soy sauce, honey, mustard, garlic and ginger together in a small bowl or jug.

2 Place the strips of steak in a non-metallic bowl and pour over the soy and honey mixture. Leave to marinate for at least 20 minutes.

3 Meanwhile, toss together the spring onions, carrot, cucumber and mangetout.

4 Preheat a griddle pan to hot, add the steak strips and cook for 1–2 minutes, pouring the remaining marinade into the pan at the end of cooking to heat through.

5 Divide the steak between the lettuce leaves, then top with the salad ingredients, finishing with a sprig of coriander and sprinkling of sesame seeds, if you like. Drizzle over a little cooked marinade, if liked.

LEMON CHICKEN COURGETTI

Serves: 4   **Prep: 10 mins**   **Cook: 8 mins**

Ingredients

2 green courgettes

2 yellow courgettes

2½ tbsp olive oil

2 large chicken breast fillets, cut crossways into 10 slices

1 tsp crushed coriander seeds

1 tsp crushed cumin seeds

½ tsp sea salt

½ tsp pepper

juice of 1 lemon

2 tbsp pine nuts, toasted

3 tbsp fresh coriander leaves

Method

1. Using a spiralizer, the side of a box grater or vegetable peeler, slice the courgettes into spiral or thin ribbons.

2. Add ½ tablespoon of the oil to a non-stick frying pan and place over a high heat. Fry the chicken slices for 1–2 minutes, or until lightly flecked with golden brown, turning once or twice. Turn the heat down to medium and add half of the remaining oil, the seeds, salt, pepper and half of the lemon juice.

3. Cook, stirring occasionally, for 5 minutes, or until the chicken slices are cooked through. Check that the centre of the chicken is no longer pink.

4. Meanwhile, heat the remaining oil in another large frying pan, add the courgette spirals and stir for 1–2 minutes, or until just tender and turning golden. Serve the chicken on the courgetti and scatter over the remaining lemon juice, pine nuts and coriander leaves.

SCALLOPS WITH PEA PURÉE

Serves: 4   **Prep: 20 mins**   **Cook: 15 mins**

Ingredients

0 g/1 lb 2 oz frozen peas

arge handfuls fresh mint
eaves, roughly chopped

150 g/5½ oz butter

12 fat scallops, roes
ttached, if possible, and
emoved from their shells

t and pepper (optional)

Method

1 Bring a large saucepan of water to the boil, then add the peas. Bring back to the boil and simmer for 3 minutes. Drain the peas, then put them in a food processor or blender with the mint, 100 g/3½ oz of the butter and a large pinch of salt. Process to a smooth purée, adding a little hot water if the mixture needs loosening. Taste for seasoning, cover and keep warm.

2 Pat the scallops dry, then season them well with salt and pepper, if using.

3 Place a large frying pan over a high heat and add the remaining butter. When the butter starts to smoke, add the scallops and sear them for 1–2 minutes on each side. They should be brown and crisp on the outside but light and moist in the middle. Remove the pan from the heat.

4 Spread a spoonful of pea purée on each of four plates and place three scallops on top of each. Season and serve immediately.

LUNCHES

PESTO SALMON WITH SPRING VEG BOWL

Serves: 4 **Prep: 15 mins** **Cook: 10–12 mins**

Ingredients

200 g/7 oz fresh or frozen peas

200 g/7 oz fresh broad beans

200 g/7 oz asparagus, woody stems discarded

200 g/7 oz baby carrots, scrubbed

4 skinless salmon fillets, each weighing 150 g/5½ oz

4 tbsp pesto

3 tbsp extra virgin olive oil

grated rind and juice of 1 lemon

2 tbsp sunflower seeds, toasted

2 tbsp pumpkin seeds, toasted

2 tbsp shredded fresh basil

Method

1 Place all the vegetables in a steamer and cook for 10–12 minutes, until tender.

2 Meanwhile, preheat the grill to hot and line a baking sheet with foil. Place the salmon on the prepared baking sheet and spoon over the pesto. Cook under the grill for 3–4 minutes on each side.

3 Mix the oil with the lemon rind and juice and toss with the cooked vegetables.

4 Divide the vegetables between four warmed shallow bowls and top each one with a salmon fillet.

5 Sprinkle with the sunflower seeds, pumpkin seeds and shredded basil and serve.

★ Variation

If you need a more filling dish just add a little cooked gluten-free pasta for extra energy-giving carbohydrates.

LUNCHES

TUNA & WASABI BURGERS
WITH PICKLED VEGETABLES

Serves: 4

Prep: 40 mins
plus cooling

Cook: 15 mins

Ingredients

4 tbsp rice wine vinegar

1 tbsp caster sugar

125 ml/4 fl oz water

½ tsp coriander seeds, crushed and ½ tsp mustard seeds

½ cucumber, sliced

2 carrots, cut into ribbons

6 radishes, thinly sliced

3 shallots, thinly sliced

Tuna & wasabi burgers

400 g/14 oz tuna steaks, sliced into 2.5-cm/1-inch pieces

25 g/1 oz fresh coriander, finely chopped

zest and juice of 1 lime

2 tsp gluten-free wasabi paste

4 spring onions, finely chopped

2 tbsp gluten-free mayonnaise

Lime crème fraîche

4 tbsp crème fraîche

zest and juice of 1 lime

Method

1 To make the pickled vegetables, heat the vinegar, sugar and water in a small pan over a medium heat. Let the sugar dissolve and bring to a gentle simmer. Remove from the heat and add the coriander seeds and mustard seeds.

2 Put the cucumber, carrots, radishes and shallots in a small bowl or sterilized jar and pour over the pickling liquid. Leave to pickle overnight, or for a least 4 hours.

3 Briefly pulse the tuna slices in a food processor until just chopped. Transfer to a large bowl and combine with the coriander, lime zest, lime juice, wasabi paste, spring onions and mayonnaise. Mix well and chill in the fridge for 15 minutes.

4 Meanwhile, make the lime crème fraîche. Combine the crème fraiche, lime zest and juice to taste in a bowl. Set aside.

5 Shape the tuna mixture into 4 burgers and brush each one with oil. Griddle them for 6 minutes on each side, or until the burgers are cooked through.

6 Serve the burgers with the pickled vegetables and a dollop of lime crème fraîche.

SUSHI ROLL BOWL

Serves: 4

Prep: 15 mins
plus cooling

Cook: 10 mins

Ingredients

300 g/10½ oz sushi rice

2 tbsp rice vinegar

1 tsp caster sugar

1 large avocado, peeled, stoned and sliced

200 g/7 oz raw tuna, sliced

200 g/7 oz raw salmon, sliced

juice of ½ lemon

4 sheets nori seaweed, shredded

¼ cucumber, cut into matchsticks

2 tbsp snipped fresh chives

1 tbsp black sesame seeds

4 tbsp gluten-free soy sauce, to serve

Method

1 Cook the rice according to the packet instructions. When all the water has been absorbed and the rice is cooked, stir through the vinegar and sugar, then cover and leave to cool.

2 Divide the rice between four bowls.

3 Top each bowl with slices of avocado, tuna and salmon.

4 Squeeze over the lemon juice, then add the nori cucumber, chives and sesame seeds.

5 Serve with the soy sauce.

★ Variation

If you are not keen on eating raw fish then you could use smoked salmon or trout instead.

LUNCHES

BAKED SALMON WITH SWEET POTATO & CUCUMBER

Serves: 4   **Prep: 15 mins**   **Cook: 16 mins**

Ingredients

2 sweet potatoes, peeled

1½ tbsp extra virgin rapeseed oil

½ tsp sea salt

½ tsp pepper

1 cucumber, topped and tailed

1 tbsp white wine vinegar

1 tsp mild-flavoured runny honey, such as acacia

4 thick salmon fillets, about 125 g/4½ oz each

2 tsp crushed cumin seeds

1 tbsp chopped fresh dill, to garnish

Method

1 Preheat the oven to 190°C/375°F/Gas Mark 5. Slice the sweet potatoes lengthways into long, thin ribbons using a vegetable peeler or a spiralizer. Toss the ribbons in a bowl with half of the oil and half of the salt and pepper then arrange on a baking tray. Place the tray near the top of the preheated oven and cook for 6 minutes. Leave the oven on.

2 Slice the cucumber into long, thin ribbons using a vegetable peeler or a spiralizer and put the ribbons in a bowl. Combine the vinegar and honey in a small bowl, sprinkle the mixture over the cucumber and stir gently to combine.

3 Place the salmon fillets on a baking tray, brush with the remaining oil, sprinkle with the crushed cumin seeds and the rest of the salt and pepper and place in the centre of the oven. Use tongs to turn the sweet potato ribbons over and return them to the oven.

4 Bake for 10 minutes, until the salmon is cooked through and the potato ribbons are tender and turning golden.

5 Serve the salmon with the potato ribbons and the dressed cucumber ribbons on the side. Garnish with the chopped dill.

LUNCHES

MAIN MEALS

PEA & SPROUTING SEEDS BUCKWHEAT POWER BOWL

Serves: 4

Prep: 10 mins
plus cooling

Cook: 20 mins

Ingredients

4 carrots, cut into quarters lengthways

2½ tbsp extra virgin rapeseed oil

1½ tbsp maple syrup

100 g/3½ oz ready-roasted buckwheat groats

250 g/9 oz mixed sprouted seeds (such as aduki beans, alfalfa, radish and lentil)

¼ cucumber, diced

2 celery sticks, diced

1 red-skinned apple, diced

4 spring onions, diced

60 g/2¼ oz cooked small peas

juice of 1 orange

juice of ½ lemon

½ tsp sea salt

½ tsp pepper

30 g/1 oz pea shoots

Method

1 Preheat the oven to 190°C/375°F/Gas Mark 5.

2 Toss the carrots in ½ tablespoon of the oil and in ½ tablespoon of the maple syrup. Roast in the preheated oven for 20 minutes, or until golden and just tender. Leave to cool.

3 Meanwhile, pour the groats into 175 ml/6 fl oz of boiling water in a large saucepan. Stir and bring to the boil, then reduce to a simmer, put a lid on and cook for 10 minutes, or until the groats are cooked. Turn the heat off and let the pan stand on the heat for a few minutes with the lid on, then tip into a serving bowl and leave to cool.

4 Mix the cooled groats with the sprouted seeds, cucumber, celery, apple, spring onions and peas.

5 Combine the remaining rapeseed oil and maple syrup with the orange and lemon juices and salt and pepper in a small bowl. Stir this dressing into the buckwheat mixture. Top with the roasted carrots and pea shoots, then serve in individual bowls.

MUSHROOM PASTA

Serves: 4   **Prep: 15 mins**   **Cook: 25–30 mins**

Ingredients

300 g/10½ oz dried
gluten-free penne or pasta
shape of your choice

2 tbsp olive oil

250 g/9 oz
mushrooms, sliced

1 tsp dried oregano

250 ml/9 fl oz gluten-free
vegetable stock

1 tbsp lemon juice

6 tbsp cream cheese

200 g/7 oz frozen
spinach leaves

salt and pepper (optional)

Method

1 Cook the pasta in a large saucepan of lightly salted boiling water according to the packet instructions. Drain, reserving 175 ml/6 fl oz of the cooking liquid.

2 Meanwhile, heat the oil in a large, heavy-based frying pan over a medium heat, add the mushrooms and cook, stirring frequently, for 8 minutes, or until almost crisp. Stir in the oregano, stock and lemon juice and cook for 10–12 minutes, or until the sauce is reduced by half.

3 Stir in the cream cheese and spinach and cook over a medium–low heat for 3–5 minutes. Add the reserved cooking liquid, then the cooked pasta. Stir well, season to taste with salt and pepper and heat through before serving.

JAMAICAN RICE PEAS WITH TOFU

Serves: 4   **Prep: 15 mins**   **Cook: 15–20 mins**

Ingredients

250 g/9 oz firm plain tofu, cubed

2 tbsp chopped fresh thyme, plus extra sprigs to garnish

2 tbsp olive oil

1 onion, sliced

1 garlic clove, crushed

1 small fresh red chilli, chopped

400 ml/14 fl oz gluten-free stock

200 g/7 oz basmati rice

4 tbsp coconut cream

400 g/14 oz canned red kidney beans, drained and rinsed

salt and pepper (optional)

Method

1 Toss the tofu with half the chopped thyme and sprinkle with salt and pepper, to taste, if using.

2 Heat 1 tablespoon of the oil in a large pan, add the tofu and fry, stirring occasionally, for 2 minutes. Remove and keep warm.

3 Add the remaining oil to the pan, then add the onion and fry, stirring, for 3–4 minutes. Stir in the garlic, chilli and the remaining chopped thyme then add the stock and bring to the boil. Stir in the rice, then reduce the heat, cover and simmer for 12–15 minutes, until the rice is tender.

4 Stir in the coconut cream and beans, season to taste with salt and pepper and cook gently for 2–3 minutes. Spoon the tofu over the rice and serve hot, garnished with thyme sprigs.

PUMPKIN & CHESTNUT RISOTTO

Serves: 4　　　　**Prep: 20 mins**　　　　**Cook: 35–40 mins**

Ingredients

1 tbsp olive oil

40 g/1½ oz butter

1 small onion,
finely chopped

225 g/8 oz pumpkin, diced

225 g/8 oz chestnuts,
cooked and shelled

280 g/10 oz risotto rice

150 ml/5 fl oz gluten-free
dry white wine

1 tsp crumbled saffron
threads (optional),
dissolved in 4 tbsp
of the stock

1 litre/1¾ pints simmering
gluten-free vegetable stock

85 g/3 oz freshly grated
Parmesan cheese, plus
extra for serving

salt and pepper (optional)

Method

1 Heat the oil with 25 g/1 oz of the butter in a saucepan over a medium heat until the butter has melted. Stir in the onion and pumpkin and cook, stirring occasionally, for 5 minutes, until the onion is soft and the pumpkin begins to colour.

2 Roughly chop the chestnuts and add to the mixture. Stir thoroughly to coat.

3 Reduce the heat, add the rice and mix to coat in oil and butter. Cook, stirring constantly, for 2–3 minutes. Add the wine and cook, stirring constantly, for 1 minute, until it has reduced.

4 Add the saffron liquid to the rice, if using, and cook, stirring, until the liquid has been absorbed. Add the simmering stock, a ladleful at a time, stirring constantly. Add more liquid as the rice absorbs each addition. Increase the heat to medium so that the liquid bubbles.

5 Cook for 20 minutes, or until all the liquid has been absorbed and the rice is creamy. Season to taste with salt and pepper, if using.

6 Remove the risotto from the heat and add the remaining butter. Mix well, then stir in the Parmesan until it melts. Spoon the risotto onto warmed plates, sprinkle with grated Parmesan and serve.

SQUASH & RED PEPPER PIE

Serves: 8

Prep: 55 mins

Cook: 1 hour 55 mins–2 hours 15 mins

Ingredients

Spiced tomato sauce

2 tbsp olive oil

1 red onion, chopped

2 large garlic cloves, finely chopped

1 tsp cumin seeds

2 x 400 g/14 oz can chopped plum tomatoes

1 tbsp soft light brown sugar

salt and pepper (optional)

Squash/red pepper pie

1 butternut squash, peeled and deseeded

3 large parsnips, scrubbed and trimmed

2 red peppers, deseeded

3 tbsp harissa paste

1 tbsp olive oil

1 tsp salt

20 g/½ oz fresh coriander, chopped

100 ml/3½ fl oz water

1 kg/2 lb 4 oz floury potatoes, peeled

60 ml/2 fl oz milk

1 large garlic clove, crushed

Method

1 Preheat the oven to 200°C/400°F/Gas Mark 6.

2 For the tomato sauce, heat the oil in a large, shallow casserole dish. Add the onion and cook gently for 5 minutes. Stir through the garlic and cumin and cook for 2 minutes, stirring. Pour in the tomatoes, add the sugar and season with salt and pepper, if using. Simmer for 30 minutes.

3 To make the pie, chop the squash, parsnips and peppers into 3-cm/1½-inch cubes and mix with the harissa paste, olive oil and the salt in a large bowl. Scatter the vegetables into a large, shallow roasting tin. Roast for 30 minutes, until the vegetables are beginning to caramelize.

4 Remove the roasted vegetables from the oven and mix into the tomato sauce with the coriander and water. Season with salt and pepper, if using.

5 Halve the potatoes, place them in a large saucepan and cover with cold water. Bring to the boil and simmer for 20–25 minutes. Drain well. Return the potatoes to the pan and add the milk and garlic. Mash until smooth.

6 Decant the roasted vegetable mixture into a 2-litre/3½-pint ovenproof dish and top with the mashed potato. Bake in the preheated oven for 30–40 minutes, until golden. Serve immediately.

BUCKWHEAT MUSHROOMS & ROASTED SQUASH

Serves: 4　　　　**Prep: 25 mins**　　　　**Cook: 30 mins**

Ingredients

1 kg/2 lb 4 oz squash, such as Crown Prince or Kabocha

1 tbsp gluten-free thick balsamic vinegar

125 ml/4 fl oz olive oil

½ tbsp butter

225 g/8 oz roasted buckwheat, rinsed

1 egg, lightly beaten

450 ml/15 fl oz hot gluten-free vegetable stock

1 onion, halved and sliced

250 g/9 oz small chestnut mushrooms, quartered

2 tbsp lemon juice

6 tbsp chopped fresh flat-leaf parsley

25 g/1 oz walnut halves, roughly chopped

salt and pepper (optional)

Method

1 Preheat the oven to 200°C/400°F/Gas Mark 6. Cut the squash into eight wedges, peel and deseed.

2 Put the squash into a roasting tin and toss with the vinegar and 6 tablespoons of the oil. Season well with salt and pepper, if using, and dot with the butter. Roast in the preheated oven for 25–30 minutes, until slightly caramelized.

3 Meanwhile, put the buckwheat into a frying pan. Add the egg, stirring to coat the grains. Stir over a medium heat for 3 minutes, until the egg moisture has evaporated. Add the stock and ½ teaspoon of salt, if using. Simmer for 9–10 minutes, until the grains are tender but not disintegrating. Remove from the heat.

4 Heat the remaining oil in a deep frying pan. Add the onion and fry over a medium heat for 10 minutes. Season to taste with salt and pepper, if using. Add the mushrooms and fry for 5 minutes. Stir in the buckwheat, lemon juice and most of the parsley.

5 Transfer the buckwheat mixture to four plates and arrange the squash on top. Scatter over the walnuts and the remaining parsley. Serve.

POTATO & ONION PIE

Serves: 8

Prep: 25 minutes
plus chilling & cooling

Cook: 1 hour 30 mins

Ingredients

Pastry

400 g/14 oz gluten-free plain flour, plus 10 g/¼ oz for dusting

200 g/7 oz cold unsalted butter, cubed

pinch of salt

100 ml/3½ fl oz ice-cold water

Potato filling

600 ml/1 pint double cream

200 ml/7 fl oz semi-skimmed milk

3 large garlic cloves, peeled and crushed

10 g/¼ oz butter, for greasing

1 white onion, halved and thinly sliced

1 kg/2 lb 4 oz floury potatoes, peeled and sliced as thinly as possible

1 egg, lightly beaten

salt and pepper (optional)

Method

1. Put the plain flour, cubed butter and salt in the bowl of a food processor and whizz until the mixture resembles breadcrumbs. Very slowly, pour the water into the processor until the pastry begins to clump and come together. Tip onto a floured surface and bring together using your hands. Shape into a disc, wrap and chill for at least 20 minutes.

2. Meanwhile, heat your cream, milk and garlic in a small pan. Simmer for 1–2 minutes, allowing the garlic to infuse. Remove from the heat and allow the cream to cool completely.

3. Preheat the oven to 220°C/425°F/Gas Mark 7 and place a baking tray on the centre shelf.

4. Roll out your pastry in between sheets of clingfilm to about a 3 mm depth. You should have more than enough to drape over the bottom and sides of a greased 2.5-litre/4½-pint ovenproof dish. Trim around the edges. Gather any leftover pastry and re-roll into a disc. Meanwhile, fill your uncooked pasty case.

5. Cover the bottom of the pastry with the slices of potato and onion, overlapping them as you go. Season well with salt and pepper, if using, then continue to layer until all the potato and onion has been used.

MAIN MEALS

6 Slowly pour the garlicky cream mixture over the pastry, potato and onion, allowing each addition to disappear between the layers before adding more. Season again.

7 Re-roll the pastry to fit the top of the dish. Brush the exposed edges with egg and place the pastry on the top. Make a little hole, 1 cm/½ inch in diameter, on the surface of the pastry and brush once more with the beaten egg.

8 Place the pie on the baking sheet and cook for 15 minutes before reducing the oven temperature to 160°C/325°F/Gas Mark 3. Bake for a further 1 hour and 15 minutes. Allow the pie to sit for 10 minutes or so before serving.

QUINOA WITH ROASTED VEGETABLES

Serves: 2 **Prep: 30 mins** **Cook: 50–55 mins**

Ingredients

2 peppers, deseeded and cut into chunks

1 large courgette, cut into chunks

1 small fennel bulb, cut into thin wedges

1 tbsp olive oil

2 tsp finely chopped fresh rosemary leaves and 1 tsp chopped fresh thyme

100 g/3½ oz quinoa

350 ml/12 fl oz gluten-free vegetable stock

2 garlic cloves, peeled and crushed

3 tbsp chopped fresh flat-leaf parsley

40 g/1½ oz pine nuts, toasted

salt and pepper (optional)

Method

1 Preheat the oven to 200°C/400°F/Gas Mark 6. Place the peppers, courgette and fennel in a roasting tin large enough to hold the vegetables in a single layer.

2 Drizzle the oil over the vegetables and scatter with the rosemary and thyme. Season well with salt and pepper, if using, and mix well with your hands. Roast in the preheated oven for 25–30 minutes, until tender and lightly charred.

3 Meanwhile, place the quinoa, stock and garlic in a saucepan. Bring to the boil, cover and simmer for 12–15 minutes, until tender and most of the stock has been absorbed.

4 Remove the vegetables from the oven. Tip the quinoa into the roasting tin. Add the parsley and pine nuts and toss together. Serve warm or cold.

MAIN MEALS

QUINOA STUFFED AUBERGINES

Serves: 2　　　　**Prep: 15 mins**　　　　**Cook: 45 mins**

Ingredients

2 aubergines (about 950 g/2 lb 2 oz in total)

1 tbsp olive oil

1 small onion, diced

2 garlic cloves, finely chopped

135 g/4¾ oz white quinoa, rinsed

350 ml/12 fl oz gluten-free vegetable stock

1 tsp salt

pinch of pepper

2 tbsp flaked almonds, toasted

3 tbsp finely chopped fresh mint

85 g/3 oz feta cheese, crumbled

Method

1 Preheat the oven to 230°C/450°F/Gas Mark 8. Place the aubergines on a baking tray and bake in the preheated oven for 15 minutes, or until soft. Remove from the oven and leave to cool slightly.

2 Meanwhile, heat the oil in a large, heavy-based frying pan over a medium–high heat. Add the onion and garlic and cook, stirring occasionally, for about 5 minutes, or until soft. Add the quinoa, stock, salt and pepper.

3 Cut each aubergine in half lengthways and scoop out the flesh, leaving a 5 mm/¼ inch thick border inside the skin so they hold their shape.

4 Chop the aubergine flesh and stir it into the quinoa mixture in the frying pan. Reduce the heat to low–medium, cover and cook for about 15 minutes, or until the quinoa is cooked through. Remove from the heat and stir in the flaked almonds, 2 tablespoons of the mint and half the cheese.

5 Divide the quinoa mixture equally between the aubergine skins and top with the remaining cheese. Bake for about 10–15 minutes, or until the cheese is bubbling and beginning to brown. Garnish with the remaining mint and serve.

MAIN MEALS

SWEET POTATO & LENTIL STEW

Serves: 4   **Prep: 15–20 mins**   **Cook: 30 mins**

Ingredients

2 tbsp olive oil

350 g/12 oz sweet potato,
cut into 1-cm/½-inch cubes

1 onion, chopped

1 carrot, chopped

1 leek, sliced

1 bay leaf

85 g/3 oz Puy lentils

750 ml/1¼ pints
gluten-free stock

1 tbsp chopped fresh sage

salt and pepper (optional)

Method

1 Heat the oil in a large saucepan or stockpot
over a low heat. Gently fry the sweet potato,
onion, carrot, leek and bay leaf for 5 minutes.

2 Stir in the lentils, stock and sage, and bring to
the boil. Reduce the heat and simmer for
20 minutes, or until the lentils are tender but not
disintegrating.

3 Season to taste with salt and pepper, if using,
then remove and discard the bay leaf.
Serve immediately.

SICHUAN MIXED VEGETABLES

Serves: 4　　　　　**Prep: 20 mins**　　　　　**Cook: 25 mins**

Ingredients

2 tbsp chilli oil

4 garlic cloves, crushed

5-cm/2-inch piece fresh ginger, grated

250 g/9 oz carrots, cut into thin strips

1 red pepper, cut into thin strips

150 g/5½ oz shiitake mushrooms, sliced

150 g/5½ oz mangetout, halved diagonally

3 tbsp gluten-free soy sauce

3 tbsp peanut butter

350 g/12 oz beansprouts

cooked rice, to serve

Method

1 Heat the oil in a preheated wok, add the garlic, ginger and carrots and fry for 3 minutes. Add the red pepper and stir-fry for a further 2 minutes.

2 Add the mushrooms and mangetout and stir-fry for 1 minute.

3 In a small bowl, mix the soy sauce and peanut butter together until combined.

4 Using a wooden spoon, make a space in the centre of the stir-fried vegetables so that the base of the wok is visible. Pour in the sauce and bring to the boil, stirring constantly, until it starts to thicken. Add the beansprouts and toss the vegetables to coat thoroughly with the sauce.

5 Transfer to a warmed serving dish and serve immediately with the rice.

MAIN MEALS

CAULIFLOWER & BUTTER BEAN STEW

Serves: 4   **Prep: 10 mins**   **Cook: 35 mins**

Ingredients

2 tbsp olive oil

2 large red onions, sliced

2 carrots, cut into
2-cm/¾-inch dice

2 celery sticks, cut into
2-cm/¾-inch dice

3 garlic cloves, crushed

400 g/14 oz canned plum
tomatoes in juice

250 ml/9 fl oz gluten-free
vegetable stock

1 tbsp sun-dried
tomato paste

½ tbsp dried mixed herbs

½ tsp pepper

2 x 400 g/14 oz canned
butter beans, drained and
rinsed

1 head of cauliflower,
broken into florets

1 tsp sweet paprika

salt (optional)

Method

1 Add the oil to a large lidded saucepan and place over a medium–hot heat. Add the onions, carrots and celery and cook for 5 minutes, or until lightly coloured, stirring from time to time. Stir in the garlic and cook for a minute.

2 Add the canned tomatoes and their juice roughly crushing any whole ones against the sides of the pan. Stir in the stock, tomato paste, herbs, pepper and salt, if using. Bring to a simmer, reduce the heat to low and place the lid on. Cook for 20 minutes, or until the vegetables are all tender.

3 Stir in the butter beans and cook for a further 5 minutes. Place the cauliflower florets on top of the stew, put the lid back on and simmer for 5 minutes more, or until the cauliflower is just tender when the stalks are pierced with a sharp knife.

4 Serve the stew immediately, garnished with the sweet paprika.

ROAST SALMON WITH BEETROOT & HORSERADISH

Serves: 4　　　　**Prep: 30 mins**　　　　**Cook: 1 hour 15 mins**

Ingredients

250 g/9 oz green lentils, rinsed

4 tbsp olive oil

1 tbsp white wine vinegar

450 g/1 lb beetroot, cut into wedges

2 banana shallots, quartered

2 garlic cloves, lightly bashed

30 g/1 oz fresh dill, finely chopped

4 x 125 g/4½ oz salmon fillets

1 lemon, quartered

salt and pepper (optional)

Horseradish crème fraîche

1½ tbsp fresh horseradish, finely grated

125 ml/4 fl oz crème fraîche

salt and pepper (optional)

Method

1 Preheat the oven to 200°C/400°F/Gas Mark 6.

2 In a large saucepan, place the lentils and enough water to cover. Bring to a boil and reduce to a simmer. Cook for 15–20 minutes, until al dente. Then stir through 2 tablespoons of the olive oil and the white wine vinegar. Season to taste with salt and pepper, if using.

3 Place the beetroot, shallots, garlic, half of the dill and 1 tablespoon of the olive oil in a medium-sized roasting tin. Roast in the oven for 30–35 minutes, or until the beetroot is tender.

4 Combine the warm lentils with the roast beetroot mixture and spoon into a 2-litre/3½-pint ovenproof dish. Place the salmon on top, skin side up. Add the lemon and drizzle over the remaining oil. Season with salt and pepper, if using. Lower the oven temperature to 180°C/350°F/Gas Mark 4 and bake for 15–20 minutes.

5 Combine the horseradish and crème fraîche and season to taste with salt and pepper, if using. Divide the lentils and salmon between four plates and top with the horseradish crème fraîche and the remaining dill.

COCONUT FISH CURRY

Serves: 4 **Prep: 20 mins** **Cook: 20–25 mins**

Ingredients

Curry paste

3 shallots, chopped and 1 large red chilli, chopped

30 g/1 oz fresh coriander

2 garlic cloves, chopped

2 tbsp grated fresh ginger

25 g/1 oz cashew nuts, toasted

Curry

3 tbsp sunflower oil

1 red pepper, sliced

1 tsp ground turmeric, ½ tsp ground cumin, ½ tsp ground coriander and ½ tsp hot chilli powder

5 curry leaves

1 x 400 ml/14 fl oz can coconut milk and 1 x 150 ml/5 fl oz can coconut cream

50 ml/1¾ fl oz water

1 x 400 g/14 oz can chickpeas, drained and rinsed

100 g/3½ oz baby spinach

200 g/7 oz raw prawns, peeled and deveined

200 g/7 oz skinned cod fillet, cut into chunks

2 tsp mustard seeds

juice of 1 lime

Method

1 In the small bowl of a food processor, whizz together the shallots, red chilli, half of the coriander, garlic, ginger and cashew nuts until you have a smooth aromatic paste.

2 In a large heavy-based pan, heat the sunflower oil over a medium heat. Once hot, add the sliced peppers and fry for 5 minutes, or until they begin to soften. Add the curry paste and fry gently for 3 minutes. Add the turmeric, cumin, coriander and chilli powder. Fry for a further minute.

3 Add the curry leaves, coconut milk, coconut cream and water. Raise the heat and bring to the boil then lower the heat and simmer for 10–15 minutes. Add the chickpeas and cook for a further 5 minutes.

4 Add the spinach, prawns and cod to the pan and poach for 2–3 minutes.

5 Garnish with the mustard seeds, lime juice and remaining coriander. Serve immediately.

MONKFISH & BROCCOLI COCONUT CURRY

Serves: 4　　　　**Prep: 15 mins**　　　　**Cook: 20 mins**

Ingredients

1 large onion, chopped

2 tsp gluten-free fish sauce

juice of ½ lime

1 red chilli, de-stalked and
1 red chilli, chopped

1 green chilli, de-stalked

2 tsp crushed coriander
seeds

2 tsp crushed cumin seeds

2.5-cm/1-inch piece fresh
ginger, chopped

3 garlic cloves, roughly
chopped

½ lemon grass stalk

1½ tbsp groundnut oil

5 curry leaves

300 ml/10 fl oz full-fat
coconut milk

350 g/12 oz purple
sprouting broccoli, each
spear cut into 2 pieces

500 g/1 lb 2 oz monkfish
fillet, cubed

Method

1 Add the onion, fish sauce, lime juice, destalked chillies, seeds, ginger, garlic, lemon grass and half of the oil to the bowl of a blender or food processor and process until you have a paste. Tip the mixture into a frying pan and cook over a medium heat for 2 minutes. Stir in the curry leaves and coconut milk and simmer for 10 more minutes.

2 Meanwhile, add the remaining oil to another frying pan and place over a high heat. Stir-fry the broccoli for 2 minutes, or until just tender. Set aside.

3 Add the monkfish cubes to the curry pan and bring back to a simmer. Cook for 2 minutes, then add the broccoli spears to the pan and continue cooking for a further minute. Serve the curry with the remaining chopped chilli sprinkled over the top.

GRILLED SEA BASS WITH FRIED QUINOA

Serves: 2   **Prep: 20 mins**   **Cook: 40 mins**

Ingredients

225 ml/8 fl oz water

85 g/3 oz white quinoa, rinsed

2 whole sea bass, about 350 g/12 oz each, scaled and gutted, heads removed

2 tsp fennel seeds, crushed

½ preserved lemon, roughly chopped

3 tbsp olive oil

6 tbsp chopped fresh flat-leaf parsley

1 tbsp olive oil, for brushing

salt and pepper (optional)

1 lemon, cut into wedges, to garnish

Method

1. Put the water and quinoa into a saucepan and bring to the boil. Cover and simmer over a very low heat for 10 minutes. Remove from the heat, but leave the pan covered for a further 10 minutes to allow the grains to swell. Fluff up with a fork and spread out on a tray to dry.

2. Make two slashes on each side of the fish. Combine the fennel seeds, preserved lemon, ¼ teaspoon of salt and ¼ teaspoon of pepper. Stuff the mixture into the slits.

3. Tip the quinoa into a 28–30 cm/11–12 inch frying pan. Place over a medium–high heat and sprinkle with the oil. Fry for 2 minutes, then reduce the heat to medium and cook for a further 15 minutes, stirring, until slightly crispy. Stir in the parsley and season to taste with salt and pepper, if using. Set aside and keep warm until ready to serve.

4. Preheat the grill. Line a baking tray with aluminium foil. Brush the fish generously with oil and place on the prepared tray. Place under the preheated grill and cook for 4–5 minutes on each side, until the flesh is opaque.

5. Divide the quinoa between two plates. Place the fish on top, garnish with lemon wedges and serve immediately.

BRIGHT GREEN MACKEREL & BUTTER BEANS

Serves: 4   **Prep: 20 mins**   **Cook: 35–40 mins,**

Ingredients

2 tbsp olive oil

5 shallots, sliced

3 garlic cloves, sliced

150 g/5½ oz tenderstem broccoli

x 400 g/14 oz cans butter beans, drained and rinsed

2 courgettes, grated

100 ml/3½ fl oz luten-free vegetable stock

100 ml/3½ fl oz double cream

10 g/¼ oz fresh basil, torn

4 x 90 g/3¼ oz mackerel llets, deboned but skin on

alt and pepper (optional)

Method

1 Preheat the oven to 180°C/350°F/Gas Mark 4.

2 Heat half of the olive oil in a medium-sized deep frying pan over a high heat. Add the shallots and garlic and fry for 3–4 minutes until golden. Remove from the heat and set aside.

3 Bring a pan of water to the boil and add the broccoli. Simmer for 5–6 minutes, until it has just started to soften. Drain and set aside.

4 Transfer the shallots, garlic, butter beans, courgette, vegetable stock, cream, half of the torn basil and softened broccoli to a 2-litre/ 3½-pint ovenproof dish and mix well. Cover with foil and transfer to the oven for 20 minutes.

5 Heat the remaining oil in a large non-stick frying pan over a high heat. Once hot, place the mackerel fillets in the pan skin side down, gently applying pressure to the skin, and fry for 3 minutes, until the skin is crispy. Remove the fillets from the pan without cooking the flesh side.

6 Remove the vegetables from the oven and take off the foil. Place the fillets over the bean mixture, skin side up. Season with salt and pepper to taste, if using, and return to the oven for 4–5 minutes, until the mackerel is cooked. Serve, garnished with the remaining basil.

MAIN MEALS

ITALIAN RICE WITH CHICKEN & CHERRY TOMATOES

Serves: 6   **Prep: 20 mins**   **Cook: 1 hour**

Ingredients

250 g/9 oz brown rice, rinsed

6 boneless chicken thighs (about 550 g/1 lb 4 oz)

2 tbsp olive oil

1 red onion, sliced

3 fresh thyme sprigs

juice and zest of 1 lemon

3 garlic cloves, bashed

200 g/7 oz cherry tomatoes

50 g/1¾ oz black olives, stoned and chopped

15 g/½ oz fresh basil, chopped

125 g/4½ oz buffalo mozzarella, torn

40 g/1½ oz freshly grated Parmesan cheese

40 g/1½ oz pine nuts

salt and pepper (optional)

Method

1 Preheat the oven to 180°C/350°F/Gas Mark 4.

2 Bring a large pan of water to the boil over a high heat. Lower the heat and add the brown rice. Cook for 25–30 minutes, or until al dente.

3 Using a medium-sized roasting dish, add the chicken thighs, 1 tablespoon of olive oil, the red onion, half of the thyme, the lemon juice, lemon zest and garlic. Season with salt and pepper, if using, and cook for 10 minutes.

4 Baste the chicken with the olive oil and lemon juice. Add the tomatoes to the roasting dish and cook for a further 10 minutes, until the chicken is tender and the juices run clear when a skewer is inserted into the thickest part of the meat. Remove the roasting dish from the oven and allow the chicken to cool.

5 Strain the rice. Mix it with the cooking juices, the onion, tomatoes, olives and basil.

6 Raise the oven temperature to 200°C/400°F/Gas Mark 6. Spoon the rice mixture into a medium-sized ovenproof dish and nestle the chicken thighs into the rice. Top with the mozzarella and Parmesan. Sprinkle the pine nuts over, and drizzle with the remaining oil. Bake for 10 minutes, or until the mozzarella is golden and bubbling.

CREOLE CHICKEN WITH CORIANDER PARSNIP RICE

Serves: 4   **Prep: 15 mins**   **Cook: 25 mins**

Ingredients

2 tbsp extra virgin rapeseed oil

4 small chicken breast fillets, each sliced into 3 equal pieces

1 large onion, sliced

2 celery sticks, finely chopped

1 green pepper, deseeded and thinly sliced

1 yellow pepper, deseeded and thinly sliced

2 garlic cloves, crushed

1 tsp smoked paprika

300 g/10½ oz canned chopped tomatoes

1 tsp sea salt

1 tsp pepper

2 large parsnips, roughly chopped

1 tbsp raw hemp seeds

4 tbsp fresh coriander leaves

4 fresh coriander sprigs, to garnish

Method

1 Heat half of the oil in a large frying pan over a high heat. Add the sliced chicken pieces and fry for 2 minutes, or until very lightly browned. Remove the chicken pieces from the pan with a slotted spatula and transfer to a plate. Set aside.

2 Add the onion, celery and peppers to the frying pan with half of the remaining oil. Turn the heat down to medium and fry, stirring frequently, for about 10 minutes, or until the vegetables have softened and are just turning golden.

3 Stir in the garlic and paprika and cook for 30 seconds. Add the chopped tomatoes and half of the salt and pepper. Return the chicken to the pan, bring to a simmer and cook for 10 minutes.

4 Meanwhile, add the parsnips to the bowl of a food processor. Process on high until they resemble rice grains then stir in the hemp seeds and the remaining salt and pepper.

5 Heat the remaining oil in a frying pan over a medium heat. Stir in the parsnip rice and stir-fry for 2 minutes, then stir through the coriander leaves. Serve the chicken mixture spooned over the parsnip rice and garnished with the coriander sprig.

CHICKEN PEPERONATA BOWL

Serves: 4   **Prep: 15 mins**   **Cook: 35 mins**

Ingredients

2 red peppers, deseeded and sliced

2 yellow peppers, deseeded and sliced

1 tbsp olive oil

2 red onions, peeled and finely sliced

300 g/10½ oz dried gluten-free penne

4 skinless chicken breasts

2 garlic cloves, crushed

50 g/1¾ oz fresh basil, chopped

2 tbsp balsamic vinegar

2 tbsp fresh Parmesan cheese shavings

salt and pepper (optional)

Method

1 To make the peperonata, place the red peppers, yellow peppers and oil in a frying pan over a medium heat. Cover and cook gently for 15 minutes.

2 Add the onions and cook for a further 15 minutes.

3 Meanwhile, cook the penne according to the packet instructions.

4 Preheat a griddle pan to hot, add the chicken breasts and cook for 6–8 minutes on each side, until cooked through.

5 Meanwhile, toss the garlic and basil into the pepper mixture, then add the vinegar and cook for 2–3 minutes.

6 Drain the penne and toss into the peperonata. Season to taste with salt and pepper, if using.

7 Slice the chicken breasts diagonally. Divide the penne between four warmed bowls. Top with the chicken and some Parmesan cheese shavings.

DUCK BREASTS
WITH PLUM SAUCE

Serves: 4 **Prep: 20 mins** **Cook: 20–25 mins, plus resting**

Ingredients

1 tbsp duck fat or sunflower oil

4 duck breasts, about 350 g/12 oz each, finely scored through the skin to the fat, cooked

French beans, to serve

Plum sauce

1 tbsp sunflower oil

1 shallot, finely chopped

1½ tbsp soft light brown sugar, plus extra, if needed

½ tsp ground ginger

4 plums, stoned and roughly chopped

4 tbsp gluten-free dry white wine

1 tsp orange juice, plus extra, if needed

salt and pepper (optional)

Method

1 Preheat the oven to 200°C/400°F/Gas Mark 6.

2 To make the sauce, heat the oil in a frying pan over a high heat. Add the shallot and cook until soft. Stir in the sugar and ginger, add the plums and season to taste with salt and pepper, if using. Stir until the sugar is dissolved and is just beginning to caramelize. Immediately add the wine and orange juice and bring to the boil, stirring.

3 Reduce the heat to low and leave to simmer until the plums are tender and beginning to fall apart and the liquid is reduced. Taste and adjust the seasoning with salt and pepper, if needed. Add extra sugar or orange juice depending on how tart or sweet the plums are. Cover the sauce and set aside until required.

4 Meanwhile, melt the duck fat or oil in a large flameproof casserole wide enough to hold all the breasts in a single layer, or use a large frying pan with an ovenproof handle.

5 Add the duck breasts, skin-side down, and fry for 3–5 minutes, or until golden brown. Turn the duck breasts skin-side up and put them in the oven for 10 minutes for medium-rare and up to 15 minutes for well done.

- Transfer the duck breasts to a chopping board, cover them and leave to rest for 5 minutes.

- Thinly slice the duck breasts diagonally and transfer to warmed plates. Add any accumulated juices to the sauce and quickly return the sauce to the boil to reheat.

- Serve immediately, with the sauce spooned over the duck breasts and the French beans alongside.

WHITE CHICKEN CHILLI

Serves: 6   **Prep: 15 mins**   **Cook: 40 mins**

Ingredients

1 tbsp vegetable oil

1 onion, diced

2 garlic cloves, finely chopped

1 green pepper, deseeded and diced

1 small green jalapeño chilli, deseeded and diced

2 tsp chilli powder

2 tsp dried oregano

1 tsp ground cumin

1 tsp salt

500 g/1 lb 2 oz canned cannellini beans, drained and rinsed

750 ml/1¼ pints gluten-free chicken stock

450 g/1 lb cooked chicken breasts, shredded

juice of 1 lime

25 g/1 oz chopped fresh coriander

Method

1 Heat the oil in a large, heavy-based saucepan over a medium–high heat. Add the onion, garlic, green pepper and chilli and cook, stirring occasionally, for about 5 minutes, or until soft.

2 Add the chilli powder, oregano, cumin and salt to the saucepan and cook, stirring, for a further 30 seconds. Add the beans and stock and bring to the boil. Reduce the heat to medium–low and simmer gently, uncovered, for about 20 minutes.

3 Ladle about half of the bean mixture into a blender or food processor and purée. Return the purée to the pan along with the shredded chicken. Simmer for about 10 minutes, or until heated through. Just before serving, stir in the lime juice and coriander. Serve immediately.

SAUSAGES WITH RED PEPPERS & GREEN LENTILS

Serves: 4 **Prep: 20 mins** **Cook: 55 mins– 1 hour 10 mins**

Ingredients

250 g/9 oz green lentils, rinsed

5 tbsp olive oil

juice of ½ lemon

2 red peppers, deseeded and halved

6 large gluten-free pork sausages (about 400 g/14 oz)

1 garlic bulb, halved

3 fresh rosemary sprigs

salt and pepper (optional)

Method

1 Preheat the oven to 200°C/400°F/Gas Mark 6.

2 Place the lentils in a large saucepan over a high heat and cover with water. Bring to a boil and reduce the heat to a simmer, cooking for 15–20 minutes, or until the lentils are al dente. Strain. Stir though 2 tablespoons of the olive oil and the lemon juice. Season to taste with salt and pepper, if using.

3 Turn the grill to the highest temperature. Place the pepper halves on a medium-sized baking tray, cut side down, and grill for 15–20 minutes, or until they are charred and completely blackened. Place in a bowl and cover with cling film. Once cool, peel off the charred skin and slice into strips.

4 Mix the peppers with the lentils and spread on a medium-sized baking tray. Place the sausages, garlic halves and rosemary sprigs on the tray. Drizzle over the remaining oil and bake for 25–30 minutes, or until the sausages are browning and cooked all the way through. Serve immediately.

★ Variation

To make a vegetarian version of this dish, switch the sausages for aubergine halves.

LAMB KOFTAS

Serves: 4

Prep: 25 mins
plus chilling

Cook: 30 mins

Ingredients

250 g/9 oz fresh lean
lamb mince

1 onion, finely chopped

1 tbsp chopped
fresh coriander

1 tbsp chopped
fresh parsley

½ tsp ground coriander

¼ tsp chilli powder

oil, for brushing

salt and pepper (optional)

Chickpea mash

1 tbsp olive oil

2 garlic cloves, chopped

400 g/14 oz canned
chickpeas, drained
and rinsed

50 ml/1¾ fl oz milk

2 tbsp chopped
fresh coriander

salt and pepper (optional)

coriander sprigs, to garnish

Method

1 You will need wooden skewers for this recipe.
Put the lamb, onion, herbs, spices and salt and
pepper to taste, if using, in a food processor.
Process until thoroughly combined.

2 Divide the mixture into 12 portions and, using
wet hands, shape each portion into a sausage
shape around a wooden skewer (soaked in
water first to prevent burning). Cover and chill
the skewers in the refrigerator for 30 minutes.

3 To cook, preheat a griddle pan over a medium
heat and brush with a little oil. Cook the
skewers in 2 batches, turning occasionally,
for 10 minutes, or until browned on all sides
and cooked through.

4 To make the chickpea mash, heat the oil in a
saucepan and gently fry the garlic for 2 minutes.
Add the chickpeas and milk and heat through
for a few minutes. Transfer to a food processor
or blender and process until smooth. Season
to taste with salt and pepper, if using, then stir
in the fresh coriander. Garnish with coriander
sprigs and serve with the koftas.

STEAK & CHIPS WITH WATERCRESS BUTTER

Serves: 4

Prep: 25 mins
plus chilling

**Cook: 45 mins–
1 hour**

Ingredients

1 bunch of watercress, plus extra to garnish

85 g/3 oz unsalted butter, softened

4 sirloin steaks, about 225 g/8 oz each

4 tsp hot pepper sauce

salt and pepper (optional)

Chips

450 g/1 lb potatoes, peeled

2 tbsp sunflower oil

Method

1 To make the chips, preheat the oven to 200°C/400°F/Gas Mark 6. Cut the potatoes into thick, even-sized chips. Rinse them under cold running water and then dry well on a clean tea towel. Place in a bowl, add the oil and toss together until coated.

2 Spread the chips in a single layer on a baking sheet and cook in the preheated oven for 40–45 minutes, turning once, or until golden.

3 Using a sharp knife, finely chop enough watercress to fill 4 tablespoons. Place the butter in a small bowl and beat in the watercress with a fork until fully incorporated. Cover with clingfilm and leave to chill until required.

4 Preheat a griddle pan to high. Sprinkle each steak with 1 teaspoon of the hot pepper sauce, rubbing it in well. Season to taste with salt and pepper, if using.

5 Cook the steaks on the preheated griddle for 2½ minutes each side for rare, 4 minutes each side for medium and 6 minutes each side for well done. Transfer to serving plates and serve immediately, topped with the watercress butter and accompanied by the chips. Garnish with watercress.

MAIN MEALS

CHIMICHURRI STEAK

Serves: 4　　**Prep: 20 mins**　　**Cook: 20 mins,**
plus resting

Ingredients

675–900 g/1 lb 8 oz–2 lb
sirloin steak

4 fresh corn cobs

1 shallot

3 garlic cloves

4 tbsp sherry vinegar
or red wine vinegar

1 tsp salt

60 g/2¼ oz fresh
flat-leaf parsley

1 tbsp fresh oregano leaves

½ tsp crushed red
pepper flakes

125 ml/4 fl oz olive oil

juice of 1 lemon

salt and pepper (optional)

Method

1 Preheat the grill to medium-high. Generously
season the steak with salt and pepper, if using.
Remove the corn husks and silks and wrap the
cobs individually in foil.

2 Finely chop the shallot and garlic and place
them in a small bowl with the vinegar and
1 teaspoon of salt. Finely chop the parsley and
oregano and add them to the vinegar mixture
along with the red pepper flakes. Whisk in the oil
until well combined. Stir in the lemon juice. Put
the corn and the steak on the grill rack. Cook
the steak, turning once, for about 4 minutes on
each side for medium-rare, until nicely seared on
the outside. Turn the corn occasionally, cooking
it for 15 minutes in total.

3 Transfer the meat to a chopping board and
leave to rest for 4 minutes. Slice it against the
grain into 5-mm/¼-inch thick slices. Serve the
meat drizzled with the sauce and with the corn
on the side.

MAIN MEALS

BEEF & BRASSICA STIR-FRY

Serves: 4   **Prep: 8 mins**   **Cook: 8–12 mins**

Ingredients

zest and juice of 1 orange

2 tbsp gluten-free soy sauce

2 tbsp sesame oil

250 g/9 oz purple sprouting broccoli, trimmed

200 g/7 oz cauliflower, broken into florets

1 tbsp coconut oil

5-cm/2-inch piece fresh ginger, peeled and shredded

1 garlic clove, peeled and sliced

1 red chilli, deseeded and diced

400 g/14 oz sirloin steak, cut into thin strips

1 red pepper, deseeded and thinly sliced

55 g/2 oz mangetout, shredded

2 tbsp sesame seeds, toasted

Method

1 Mix the orange zest and juice, soy sauce and sesame oil together in a bowl.

2 Bring a large saucepan of water to the boil, add the broccoli and cauliflower and blanch for 2 minutes, then drain.

3 Heat the coconut oil in a wok or large frying pan and add the ginger, garlic, chilli and steak and stir-fry until the steak is brown all over. Remove with a slotted spoon.

4 Add the red pepper, mangetout, broccoli and cauliflower, pour in the orange juice mixture, cover and cook for 2–3 minutes.

5 Return the steak to the wok, stir-fry for 1–2 minutes, then serve in warmed bowls, sprinkled with the toasted sesame seeds.

BEEF FRIED RICE

Serves: 6   **Prep: 15 mins**   **Cook: 30–35 mins**

Ingredients

500 g/1 lb 2 oz
long-grain rice

2 tbsp groundnut oil

4 large eggs, lightly beaten

650 g/1 lb 7 oz fresh
beef mince

1 large onion,
finely chopped

2 garlic cloves,
finely chopped

140 g/5 oz frozen peas

3 tbsp gluten-free tamari

1 tsp sugar

salt

gluten-free prawn crackers,
to serve (optional)

Method

1 Cook the rice in a large saucepan of salted boiling water for 15 minutes, until tender. Drain and rinse with boiling water. Set aside.

2 Heat a wok over a medium heat, then add the groundnut oil, swirl it around the wok and heat. Add the eggs and cook, stirring constantly, for 50–60 seconds, until set. Transfer to a dish and set aside.

3 Add the beef and stir-fry, breaking it up with a wooden spoon, for 4–5 minutes, until evenly browned. Stir in the onion, garlic and peas and stir-fry for a further 3–4 minutes.

4 Add the rice, tamari, sugar and eggs and cook, stirring constantly, for a further 1–2 minutes until heated through. Serve immediately with prawn crackers, if using.

BAKING & DESSERTS

BUTTER BEAN, HONEY & ORANGE CAKE

Serves: 8   **Prep: 25 mins**   **Cook: 45 mins**

Ingredients

10 g/¼ oz butter,
for greasing

1 x 400 g/14 oz can butter
beans, drained and rinsed

175 g/6 oz caster sugar

3 eggs

150 g/5½ oz gluten-free
self-raising flour

1 tsp runny honey

zest of 2 oranges

25 g/1 oz desiccated
coconut

1 tsp gluten-free
baking powder

Coconut & orange icing

1 x 400 ml/14 fl oz can
coconut milk, chilled
overnight

55 g/2 oz gluten-free icing
sugar, sieved

zest of 1 orange

25 g/1 oz flaked almonds,
toasted

Method

1 Grease an 18 cm/7 inch cake tin and line it with baking paper. Preheat the oven to 180°C/350°F/ Gas Mark 4.

2 Pulse the butter beans with the caster sugar in a food processor before adding the eggs one at a time. Continue to pulse and add the flour and honey. Finally add the orange zest, desiccated coconut and baking powder.

3 Pour the wet mixture into the prepared tin and bake for 35–40 minutes, until the cake is golden.

4 Remove the cake tin from the oven and transfer it to a wire rack to cool.

5 To make the icing, spoon the solid coconut cream out of the can, leaving the milk behind. Place the cream in a bowl and, using electric beaters, whip for 2–3 minutes. Sift over the icing sugar and gently mix together.

6 Cut the cake in half horizontally and spread one third of the icing over the top of one half. Position the second half on top and spread over the remaining icing. Sprinkle over the orange zest and toasted almonds, and serve.

BLACK BEAN CHOCOLATE CAKE

Serves: 8

Prep: 30 mins

**Cook: 1 hour–
1 hour 10 mins,
plus cooling**

Ingredients

250 g/9 oz unsalted butter,
softened, plus 10 g/¼ oz,
for greasing

225 g/8 oz dark brown
muscovado sugar

1 x 400 g/14 oz can black
beans, drained and rinsed

3 eggs, beaten

1 tsp vanilla essence

100 g/3½ oz gluten-free
dark chocolate, melted

225 g/8 oz gluten-free
plain flour

1 tsp gluten-free
bicarbonate of soda

25 g/1 oz pure, dark
cocoa powder

175 ml/6 fl oz boiling water

Buttercream icing

225 g/8 oz unsalted
butter, softened

450 g/1 lb gluten-free
icing sugar

150 g/5½ oz gluten-free
white chocolate, chopped
and melted

3 tbsp semi-skimmed milk

25 g/1 oz gluten-free dark
chocolate, to decorate

Method

1 Preheat the oven to 190°C/375°F/Gas Mark 5.
Grease and line a 20 cm/8 inch deep cake tin.

2 Add the softened butter, sugar and black bean
into the bowl of a food processor. Whiz until a
thick paste has formed. Transfer the mixture to
a large bowl and add the eggs, beating well
after each addition. Gradually add the vanilla
essence and melted chocolate, beating well.

3 Sift the flour, bicarbonate of soda and cocoa
powder into another mixing bowl. Add a third of
this dry mixture to the wet mixture and beat well.
Pour in half of the boiling water, then half of the
remaining dry mixture and beat again. Add the
remaining water, then the remaining dry mixture.
Beat well.

4 Carefully pour the batter into the prepared tin
and bake for 30 minutes. Reduce the heat to
160°C/325°F/Gas Mark 3 and bake for a further
30–40 minutes, or until a skewer pushed into
the centre of the cake comes out almost clean.
Don't worry if it is a bit sticky – it will continue to
cook as it cools.

5 Remove the cake from the oven and leave to
cool in the tin. Once cool, transfer the cake to a
serving plate.

To make the icing, put the softened butter into a separate large bowl and sift over the icing sugar. Slowly beat together using a handheld electric whisk until fluffy and combined. Beat in the cooled white chocolate and milk.

Slice the cake in half horizontally and spread a thick layer of buttercream on the top of one half. Cover with the second half of cake and spread the remaining buttercream over the top, leaving the sides bare.

Make chocolate curls by scraping the dark chocolate against a vegetable peeler. Sprinkle these over the top of your cake before serving.

ANGEL FOOD CAKE

Serves: 10　　　　**Prep: 15 mins**　　　　**Cook: 45 mins**

Ingredients

10 g/¼ oz butter, for greasing

10 egg whites

60 g/2¼ oz white rice flour

60 g/2¼ oz tapioca flour

60 g/2¼ oz gluten-free cornflour

60 g/2¼ oz potato flour

300 g/10½ oz caster sugar

1½ tsp gluten-free cream of tartar

½ tsp vanilla essence

½ tsp salt

500 g/1 lb 2 oz bag of frozen fruits of the forest (optional)

85 g/3 oz caster sugar (optional)

gluten-free icing sugar, to decorate

Method

1 Preheat the oven to 180°C/350°F/Gas Mark 4. Grease a 20 cm/8 inch cake tin and line with baking paper.

2 Allow the egg whites to sit for approximately 30 minutes at room temperature in a large bowl. In a separate bowl, sift the white rice flour, tapioca flour, cornflour, potato flour and 175 g/6 oz of the sugar.

3 Using a food processor or mixer, mix the egg whites with the cream of tartar, vanilla essence and salt until soft peaks form. Gradually add the remaining 125 g/4½ oz of sugar until stiff peaks develop. Add the flour mixture and fold in.

4 Spoon the mixture into the prepared tin and bake in the preheated oven for approximately 45 minutes until firm to the touch and a skewer inserted in the centre comes out clean.

5 Remove from the oven and, leaving the cake in the tin, turn upside-down to cool on a wire rack. Poach the fruits of the forest, if using, with the caster sugar gently until soft. Allow to cool completely. When the cake is cool, remove from the tin and decorate with icing sugar and the drained mixed fruit, if desired.

COOKIES &
CREAM CUPCAKES

Makes: 12   **Prep: 20 mins**   **Cook: 18–20 mins**

Ingredients

250 ml/9 fl oz milk

1 tsp cider vinegar

150 g/5½ oz caster sugar

75 ml/2½ fl oz rapeseed oil

1 tsp vanilla extract

150 g/5½ oz gluten-free
plain flour

25 g/1 oz gluten-free
cocoa powder

¾ tsp gluten-free
bicarbonate of soda

½ tsp gluten-free
baking powder

70 g/2½ oz gluten-free
cookies, chopped

Topping

35 g/1¼ oz gluten-free
margarine

35 g/1¼ oz white
vegetable shortening

300 g/10½ oz gluten-free
icing sugar

¾ tsp vanilla extract

75 ml/2½ fl oz cream

35 g/1¼ oz gluten-free
cookies, chopped

Method

1 Preheat the oven to 180°C/350°F/Gas Mark 4.
   Line a 12-hole cupcake tin with paper cases.

2 Put the milk into a measuring jug, stir in the
   vinegar and set aside for a few minutes to
   curdle.

3 Put the sugar, oil and vanilla into a large mixing
   bowl and beat together. Pour in the milk and
   vinegar, mix thoroughly and then add the
   flour, cocoa powder, bicarbonate of soda and
   baking powder. Stir until the ingredients are just
   combined, then fold in the cookie crumbs.

4 Divide the mixture evenly between the paper
   cases and bake in the preheated oven for
   18–20 minutes, or until springy to the touch and
   golden. Transfer to a wire rack to cool completely
   before icing.

5 To make the topping, beat the margarine and
   vegetable shortening together, then mix in the
   icing sugar and the vanilla. Gradually add the
   cream to achieve a thick pipeable consistency.
   Pipe or spoon the icing generously over the
   cupcakes and sprinkle with cookie crumbs.

BAKING & DESSERTS

RASPBERRY & CHOCOLATE CAKE

Serves: 12 **Prep: 20-25 mins** **Cook: 45-50 mins**

Ingredients

10 g/¼ oz margarine, for greasing

300 g/10½ oz gluten-free plain flour

50 g/1¾ oz pure and dark cocoa powder

1 tsp gluten-free baking powder

1 tsp gluten-free bicarbonate of soda

½ tsp salt

300 g/10½ oz granulated sugar

375 ml/13 fl oz milk

125 ml/4 fl oz rapeseed oil

7 tbsp gluten-free seedless raspberry jam

1 tsp vanilla extract

Icing

40 ml/1½ fl oz milk

85 g/3 oz gluten-free dark chocolate, broken into small pieces

60 g/2¼ oz gluten-free icing sugar

1 tbsp maple syrup

Method

1 Preheat the oven to 180°C/350°F/Gas Mark 4. Grease a 23 cm/9 inch cake tin and line with baking paper.

2 Sift the flour, cocoa, baking powder and bicarbonate of soda into a large mixing bowl and stir in the salt and sugar. Pour the milk into a medium saucepan and add the oil, raspberry jam and vanilla extract. Place over a medium heat and whisk to combine. Stir into the dry ingredients and mix thoroughly.

3 Transfer to the prepared cake tin and bake in the preheated oven for 45 minutes, or until a skewer inserted into the centre comes out clean. Leave to cool completely on a wire rack before icing.

4 To make the icing, heat the milk in a small saucepan over a medium heat until it reaches boiling point, then drop the chocolate into the pan and stir until completely melted. Remove from the heat and whisk in the icing sugar and maple syrup. Set aside to cool before icing the cake, using a palette knife.

CHOCOLATE, CHERRY & ALMOND FUDGE BITES

Makes: 35

Prep: 10 mins
plus chilling

Cook: none

Ingredients

100 g/3½ oz unsweetened almond butter

5 tbsp coconut oil

65 g/2¼ oz raw cacao powder

6 tbsp runny honey

¼ tsp sea salt

seeds from ½ vanilla pod

65 g/2¼ oz dried cherries

Method

1 Blend the almond butter and coconut oil in a food processor for a few seconds to combine. Add the cacao powder and blend again.

2 Stir in the honey, salt and vanilla seeds and blend again. Stir in the dried cherries. Do not blend again once the cherries have gone in.

3 Line a shallow tin or tray that is approximately 13 x 10 cm/5 x 4 inches with baking paper, allowing the paper to overhang the edges by at least 5 cm/2 inches. Spoon the mixture into the tin and level the surface. Place the mixture in the freezer for about an hour, or until firm.

4 Remove the fudge from the tin by gripping the overhanging paper. Place on a chopping board and, using a sharp knife, cut into five slices lengthways. Then cut each slice into seven squares. Serve or store in an airtight container in the refrigerator.

APRICOT & COCONUT BARS

Makes: 24   **Prep: 25 mins**   **Cook: 10 mins, plus chilling**

Ingredients

450 g/1 lb gluten-free digestive biscuits

50 g/9¼ oz dried apricots

20 g/¾ oz sesame seeds

250 g/9 oz butter, plus extra for greasing

2 tbsp honey

400 ml/14 fl oz can condensed milk

30 g/1 oz desiccated coconut

0 g/¼ oz flaked almonds

Method

1 Grease a 25- x 18-cm/10- x 7-inch rectangular baking tray and line it with baking paper.

2 In a food processor blitz the biscuits on pulse until they are crushed. Set aside. Add the apricots to the processor and blitz until finely chopped.

3 Place the apricots and biscuits in a large bowl and add the sesame seeds.

4 Place the butter, honey and condensed milk in a heavy pan, cook over a low heat, stirring until the mixture is smooth and melted. Continue to cook over a low heat, stirring for 3–4 minutes or until the mixture has thickened slightly. Remove from the heat, cool slightly and then add the crushed biscuits, apricots and sesame seeds.

5 Place the mixture on the baking tray and smooth out with a palette knife to fit the tray. Sprinkle with the coconut and flaked almonds and refrigerate for 2–3 hours until set.

6 When set, cut into bars. The bars can be stored in an airtight container for up to one week.

BAKING & DESSERTS

TAHINI CARAMEL SQUARES

Makes: 16

Prep: 20 mins
plus soaking & chilling

Cook: none

Ingredients

Base

40 g/1½ oz semi-dried apples

200 g/7 oz medjool dates, stoned

100 g/3½ oz almonds

1 tsp coconut oil

¼ tsp sea salt

Caramel

100 g/3½ oz raw cashew nuts

115 g/4 oz medjool dates, stoned

4 tbsp coconut oil

2 tbsp light gluten-free tahini

3 tbsp maple syrup

Chocolate topping

4 tbsp coconut oil

4 tbsp maple syrup

2 tsp date syrup

4 tbsp raw cacao powder

½ tsp vanilla pod seeds

Method

1 Line a 15 cm/6 inch square tin with baking paper, making sure the paper overhangs the edges by 5 cm/2 inches.

2 Soak the apple pieces in water for 5 minutes, drain and add to a food processor with the other base ingredients. Pulse until the dates and nuts are chopped and the mixture is sticky and spoon it into the base of the tin and press down Chill in the freezer for at least 15 minutes.

3 For the caramel, pulse the nuts and dates in a food processor until you have a fairly smooth mixture. Add the oil, tahini and maple syrup and process to a smooth paste. If necessary, to make a paste of dropping consistency, add 1–2 tablespoons of water and process again. Smooth the caramel on top of the base in the tin and return to the freezer for 1 hour.

4 For the chocolate topping, heat the oil and syrups in a small pan over a medium–low heat and stir in the cacao powder and vanilla seeds. Keep stirring until you have a glossy sauce. Pour this over the cold caramel and return to the freezer for 1 hour, or until the topping is firm.

5 Remove the mixture from the tin, put on a board and cut into 16 squares. Store in an airtight container in the refrigerator for up to 7 days.

MINI CHERRY PIES

Makes: 12

Prep: 30 mins
plus chilling

Cook: 35–40 mins

Ingredients

Pastry

450 g/1 lb gluten-free self-raising flour, plus extra for dusting

½ tsp xanthan gum

40 g/1½ oz gluten-free icing sugar

125 g/4½ oz butter, plus extra for greasing

125 ml/4 fl oz milk, plus extra for glazing

1 egg, beaten

Filling

675 g/1 lb 8 oz frozen or fresh cherries, stoned

300 g/10½ oz caster sugar, plus extra for sprinkling

2 tbsp gluten-free plain flour

3 tbsp gluten-free cornflour

juice and zest of 1 lemon

Method

1 Preheat the oven to 190°C/375°F/Gas Mark 5. Grease a 12-hole muffin tray.

2 To make the pastry, sift the flour, xanthan gum and icing sugar into a bowl. Rub in the butter until the mixture resembles fine breadcrumbs, then add the milk and egg (reserving some of the egg for glazing), and combine to make the pastry dough. Wrap the pastry in clingfilm and chill in the refrigerator for 30 minutes.

3 On a floured surface roll out the pastry to a thickness of 3 mm/⅛ inch and, using a 9 cm/3½ inch round cookie cutter, cut out 12 rounds to fit the prepared muffin tray. Press the pastry rounds into shape in the muffin tray.

4 In a bowl, combine the cherries, caster sugar, flour, cornflour and the juice and zest of the lemon. Divide the cherry mixture between the pastry cases. Roll out the remaining pastry and cut into 1 cm/½ inch wide strips and use to make a criss-cross lattice on top of the cherry filling, securing it at the edges with beaten egg.

5 Brush each pie with milk and sprinkle a little caster sugar on top. Bake in the preheated oven for 35–40 minutes until golden-brown on top. Remove from the oven and leave to cool in the tray for at least 1 hour before serving.

BAKING & DESSERTS

HONEY & LEMON CORN MUFFINS

Makes: 12   **Prep: 15 mins**   **Cook: 18–20 mins**

Ingredients

125 g/4½ oz gluten-free plain flour

120 g/4¼ oz gluten-free cornmeal

55 g/2 oz caster sugar

2 tsp gluten-free baking powder

¼ tsp xanthan gum

1 egg

juice and zest of ½ lemon

50 ml/1¾ fl oz vegetable oil

225 ml/8 fl oz milk

2 tbsp honey

1 tbsp glycerine

Method

1 Preheat the oven to 180°C/350°F/Gas 4. Line a 12-hole muffin tray with paper muffin cases.

2 Place the flour, cornmeal, sugar, baking powder and xanthan gum into a bowl and mix together well.

3 In a separate bowl, mix together all the remaining liquid ingredients. Add the liquid mixture to the dry mixture and fold in gently.

4 Spoon the mixture into the muffin cases and bake the muffins in the preheated oven for 18–20 minutes until well-risen and golden. Remove from the oven and cool on a wire rack.

FRUIT & SODA BREAD

Serves: 6

Prep: 25 mins
plus standing

Cook: 25–30 mins

Ingredients

55 g/2 oz ready-to-eat
stoned prunes, chopped

55 g/2 oz ready-to-eat dried
apricots, chopped

40 g/1½ oz ready-to-eat
dried apples, chopped

40 g/1½ oz dried
cranberries

150 ml/5 fl oz apple juice

2 tbsp sunflower oil,
plus extra for greasing

450 g/1 lb gluten-free plain
white flour blend

1½ tbsp gluten-free
baking powder

2 tsp xanthan gum

¼ tsp salt

225 ml/8 fl oz milk, plus
extra for brushing

4 tbsp maple syrup

1 tbsp pumpkin seeds

Method

1 Place the prunes, apricots, apples and
cranberries in a bowl and pour over the
apple juice. Cover and leave to stand for
about 30 minutes.

2 Preheat the oven to 200°C/400°F/Gas Mark 6.
Brush a baking sheet with oil. Sift the flour, baking
powder, xanthan gum and salt into a bowl and
make a well in the centre. Mix the oil, milk and
maple syrup and add to the dry ingredients
with the fruits and juice, mixing lightly to a soft,
but not sticky, dough. Add a little more milk if the
dough feels dry.

3 Shape the dough to a smooth round on the
prepared baking sheet, flatten slightly and cut
a deep cross through the centre almost to the
base. Gently pull the wedges apart at the points.
Brush with milk and sprinkle with pumpkin seeds.

4 Bake in the preheated oven for 25–30 minutes, or
until golden brown and the base sounds hollow
when tapped.

OATMEAL & VANILLA COOKIES

Makes: 24   **Prep: 20 mins**   **Cook: 18–20 mins**

Ingredients

135 g/4¾ oz butter, plus extra for greasing

235 g/8½ oz light soft brown sugar

2 eggs, beaten

1 tbsp vanilla essence

175 g/6 oz gluten-free plain flour

1 tsp xanthan gum

1½ tsp gluten-free baking powder

235 g/8½ oz gluten-free rolled oats

175 g/6 oz gluten-free dark chocolate chips

10 g/¼ oz ground almonds

Method

1 Preheat the oven to 180°C/350°F/Gas Mark 4. Grease 1–2 baking trays and line with baking paper.

2 Cream the butter and sugar together in a bowl using a whisk or in a food processor. Slowly add the eggs and vanilla essence, then slowly add the dry ingredients to the bowl and mix until well combined.

3 Divide the mixture into 20–24 balls and place them on the baking trays. Flatten each cookie using wet fingertips and press to shape.

4 Bake in the preheated oven for 18–20 minutes until golden. Remove from the oven and leave to cool on the trays. The cookies can be stored in an airtight container for up to 1 week.

BAKING & DESSERTS

ROASTED HAZELNUT SHORTBREAD

Makes: 18   **Prep: 20 mins**   **Cook: 10–15 mins**

Ingredients

90 g/1¼ oz gluten-free icing sugar

190 g/6½ oz gluten-free plain flour, plus extra for dusting

60 g/2¼ oz gluten-free cornflour

35 g/1¼ oz chopped roasted hazelnuts

30 g/1 oz ground almonds

250 g/9 oz butter, plus extra for greasing

½ tsp vanilla essence

caster sugar, for sprinkling

Method

1 Preheat the oven to 180°C/350°F/Gas Mark 4. Grease 1–2 baking trays and line them with baking paper.

2 Put the dry ingredients into a bowl and rub in the butter and vanilla essence until the ingredients form a dough.

3 Turn out onto a floured surface and knead slightly. Roll out to a thickness of 1 cm/½ inch. Cut out 16–18 rounds using a 7 cm/2¾ inch cutter and place on the baking tray.

4 Bake in the preheated oven for 10–15 minutes until golden. Remove from the oven and dust with caster sugar while still warm. Allow to cool on a wire rack.

BAKING & DESSERTS

FRUIT & NUT BREAD
WITH MACADAMIA

Serves: 8

Prep: 10 mins
plus soaking

**Cook: 1 hour–
1 hour 30 mins**

Ingredients

200 g/7 oz mixed dried fruit

350 ml/12 fl oz black tea

10 g/¼ oz butter,
for greasing

100 g/3½ oz figs

100 g/3½ oz
macadamia nuts

zest of 1 orange

2 eggs, beaten

275 g/9¾ oz gluten-free
self-raising flour

200 g/7 oz dark soft
brown sugar

Method

1 Place the dried fruit in a bowl and pour over the tea. Cover and leave the fruit to soak overnight.

2 Preheat the oven to 180°C/350°F/Gas Mark 4. Grease a 900 g/2 lb loaf tin and line it with baking paper.

3 Add the figs, macadamia nuts, orange zest, eggs, flour and sugar to the fruit mixture and combine well.

4 Pour the mixture into the prepared tin and smooth the surface. Bake for 1–1½ hours, until a skewer comes out clean when inserted into the middle of the cake.

5 Remove from the tin and cool on a wire rack, then slice and serve with butter.

★ Variation

You can experiment with different types of tea – Earl Grey or Lapsang will taste divine.

SEVEN GRAIN BREAD

Makes: 1 loaf

Prep: 20 mins
plus rising

Cook: 40–45 mins

Ingredients

10 g/¼ oz butter, for greasing

60 g/2¼ oz amaranth flour

120 g/4¼ oz brown rice flour and 120 g/4¼ oz sorghum flour

60 g/2¼ oz gluten-free cornflour and 60 g/2¼ oz tapioca flour

20 g/¾ oz ground chia seeds and 100 g/3½ oz ground flax seeds

2 tsp xanthan gum

tsp easy-blend dried yeast

1 tsp salt

3 eggs

1 tbsp vegetable oil

2 tbsp sugar

240 ml/8½ fl oz tepid water

10 g/¼ oz sunflower seeds

Method

1 Grease a 450 g/1 lb loaf tin.

2 Combine the flours, chia seeds, flax seeds, xanthan gum, yeast and salt together in a bowl.

3 In a separate bowl, mix the eggs, vegetable oil, sugar and water together until well combined. Add the dry ingredients to the egg mixture and mix well to form a soft dough.

4 Put the dough into the prepared tin, sprinkle with the sunflower seeds and cover with a clean damp tea towel. Leave in a warm place for an hour until the dough rises. Preheat the oven to 180°C/350°F/Gas Mark 4.

5 Remove the tea towel and bake the loaf in the preheated oven for 40–45 minutes until golden brown. Remove from the oven and allow to cool in the tin. When cooled, remove from the tin.

BAKING & DESSERTS

HORSERADISH SODA BREAD

Serves: 8-10   **Prep: 20 mins**   **Cook: 45 mins**

Ingredients

500 g/1 lb 2 oz gluten-free white bread flour, plus 10 g/¼ oz for dusting

2 tsp gluten-free bicarbonate of soda

1 tsp sea salt

175 g/6 oz parsnips, peeled and grated

100 g/3½ oz mature Cheddar cheese, grated

40 g/1½ oz fresh horseradish, grated

400 ml/14 fl oz buttermilk

1–2 tbsp milk (optional)

Method

1 Preheat the oven to 200°C/400°F/Gas Mark 6.

2 Sift the flour and bicarbonate of soda into a large mixing bowl and stir in the salt, parsnip, cheese and horseradish. Make a well in the centre of the mixture and pour in the buttermilk, stirring as you go. If necessary, add 1–2 tablespoons milk to bring the mixture together; it should form a soft and slightly sticky dough.

3 Shape the dough into a round and, using a floured handle of a wooden spoon, create a cross on the surface by pushing the wooden handle roughly halfway down into your uncooked loaf. Repeat to make a cross shape.

4 Bake for 45 minutes, until the bread is cooked through. Allow it to cool slightly before serving in slices.

PLUM & HAZELNUT CRUMBLE

Serves: 6 **Prep: 15 mins** **Cook: 25 mins**

Ingredients

700 g/1 lb 9 oz ripe red plums
150 ml/5 fl oz water
75 g/2¾ oz sugar
4 thinly pared strips of orange zest

Crumble topping

115 g/4 oz unsalted butter
115 g/4 oz quinoa flour
75 g/2¾ oz gluten-free rolled oats
115 g/4 oz sugar
2 tsp vanilla extract
4 tbsp hazelnuts, toasted and chopped

Method

1 Slice the plums in half lengthways. Separate the two halves and discard the stones. Slice in half again to make quarters.

2 Arrange the plums, skin-side up, in a single layer in the base of a 25 x 19 cm/10 x 7½ inch baking dish.

3 Put the water, sugar and orange zest into a small saucepan, bring to the boil and boil for about 5 minutes, or until syrupy. Remove and discard the orange zest. Pour the syrup over the plums.

4 Preheat the oven to 190°C/375°F/Gas Mark 5. To make the crumble topping, rub the butter into the flour. Add the remaining ingredients and mix to form a crumbly dough. Add 1 tablespoon of water if the mixture seems too dry.

5 Scatter the crumble topping evenly over the plums. Bake in the preheated oven for 20 minutes, until the juices are bubbling and the plums are cooked through. Cover with foil if the topping starts to brown too quickly. Remove from the oven, spoon the crumble into bowls and serve immediately.

BLACK RICE PUDDING WITH RASPBERRY COULIS

Serves: 2　　　**Prep: 15 mins**　　　**Cook: 50 mins**

Ingredients

150 g/5½ oz black rice

1 large ripe banana, chopped

100 ml/3½ fl oz almond milk

2 tbsp agave syrup

1 tsp vanilla essence

150 g/5½ oz raspberries

1 tbsp fresh lemon juice

125 g/4½ oz natural yogurt

1 tbsp dried rose petals

25 g/1 oz pumpkin seeds

Method

1 Place the black rice in a medium-sized saucepan over a high heat, cover with water and bring to the boil. Once boiling, reduce the heat and simmer for 40–45 minutes, until just tender. Drain and allow the rice to cool.

2 Meanwhile, blitz the banana, almond milk, 1 tablespoon of the agave syrup and vanilla essence in a blender along with half of the cooked rice. Stir through the remaining rice and set aside.

3 Blend the raspberries, remaining syrup and lemon juice to form a smooth consistency.

4 Spoon the sweetened rice into the bottom of two glasses. Add a layer of the raspberry coulis and dollop over the yogurt. Serve sprinkled with the rose petals and pumpkin seeds.

PECAN PIE

Serves: 12

Prep: 40 mins
plus chilling

Cook: 50–55 mins

Ingredients

Pastry

200 g/7 oz gluten-free
plain flour, sifted

25 g/1 oz rice flour

2 tbsp gluten-free
icing sugar

½ tsp xanthan gum

¼ tsp of salt

115 g/4 oz butter,
plus extra for greasing

1 egg, beaten

2 tbsp cold water

Filling

115 g/4 oz caster sugar

3 large eggs

5 tbsp golden syrup

2 tbsp Bourbon

50 g/1¾ oz butter, melted

½ tsp vanilla essence

175 g/6 oz pecan halves

vanilla ice cream, to serve

Method

1 Preheat the oven to 180°C/350°F/Gas Mark 4.
Grease a 4 cm/1½ inch deep, 23 cm/9 inch
fluted loose-based flan tin.

2 Place the flours, icing sugar, xanthan gum and
salt in a mixing bowl. Add the butter and rub in
until it resembles fine breadcrumbs.

3 Make a well in the centre of the mixture and
add the egg and a little water. Using your
hands, mix in the dry ingredients to form a
dough. Turn it out onto a floured surface and
knead well. Wrap it in clingfilm and chill in the
refrigerator for 20–30 minutes.

4 Roll out the pastry to a thickness of 3 mm/
⅛ inch and use it to line the greased flan tin. Line
the prepared pastry shell with baking paper and
baking beans and bake blind in the preheated
oven for 12 minutes until golden. Remove the
baking paper and beans.

5 For the filling, whisk the sugar and the eggs in
a bowl. Slowly stir in the golden syrup, Bourbon,
butter and vanilla essence. Scatter the pecans
over the cooked pastry base. Pour the filling over
the nuts and return to the oven. Bake for 35–40
minutes until just golden. Remove from the oven.
Serve warm or cold with vanilla ice cream.

PUMPKIN PIE SMOOTHIE BOWL

Serves: 4　　　**Prep: 15 mins**　　　**Cook: 12–15 mins**

Ingredients

800 g/1 lb 12 oz pumpkin or butternut squash, peeled, deseeded and chopped

2 bananas, chopped

1 tbsp coconut oil

½ tsp ground cinnamon

3 tbsp maple syrup

400 g/14 oz Greek-style yogurt

3 tbsp pumpkin seeds, toasted

2 tbsp sesame seeds, toasted

¼ tsp freshly grated nutmeg

Method

1　Place the pumpkin in a saucepan with some water, bring to the boil, then simmer for 12–15 minutes, until tender.

2　Drain, return to the pan and add the bananas, coconut oil, cinnamon and maple syrup. Mash to a smooth consistency.

3　Divide between four bowls and top each one with a dollop of yogurt.

4　Sprinkle with the pumpkin seeds, sesame seeds and nutmeg and serve hot or cold.

★ Variation

If pumpkins are not in season you can use butternut instead, or even sweet potato would work well – taste for sweetness when adding the maple syrup in case you need a little more with sweet potatoes.

CACAO, CHILLI & AVOCADO MOUSSE WITH BERRIES

Serves: 4

Prep: 15 mins
plus chilling

Cook: none

Ingredients

2 ripe avocados, halved
and stoned

60 g/2¼ oz cacao powder

4 tbsp agave nectar

seeds from ½ vanilla pod

½ tsp chilli powder

50 ml/1¾ fl oz canned
full-fat coconut milk

40 g/1½ oz wild
strawberries, or
small strawberries

40 g/1½ oz fresh
raspberries

½ tsp ground cinnamon

Method

1 Scoop the avocado flesh into a large bowl and mash lightly with fork.

2 Stir in the cacao powder, agave nectar, vanilla seeds and chilli powder. Blend thoroughly with a hand blender until the mixture is thick and smooth. Stir in the coconut milk and blend once again.

3 Spoon the avocado mixture into ramekins or small, stemmed glasses. Cover with clingfilm and chill for at least 4 hours.

4 Decorate the avocado mousses evenly with the berries and sprinkle the cinnamon over each dish. Serve immediately.

COCONUT RICE PUDDING WITH POMEGRANATE

Serves: 4

Prep: 15 mins
plus soaking & chilling

Cook: 45–50 mins

Ingredients

55 g/2 oz pudding rice

200 ml/7 fl oz canned light coconut milk

200 ml/7 fl oz almond milk

25 g/1 oz golden caster sugar

1 cinnamon stick

2 gelatine leaves

1 pomegranate, separated into seeds

¼ tsp freshly grated nutmeg, to sprinkle

Method

1 Place the rice, coconut milk, almond milk, sugar and cinnamon in a saucepan over a high heat. Bring almost to the boil, stirring, then reduce the heat and cover. Simmer very gently, stirring occasionally, for 40–45 minutes, or until most of the liquid is absorbed

2 Meanwhile, place the gelatine leaves in a bowl and cover with cold water. Leave to soak for 10 minutes to soften. Drain the leaves, squeezing out any excess moisture, then add to the hot rice mixture and stir lightly until completely dissolved.

3 Spoon the rice mixture into four 150-ml/5-fl oz metal pudding basins, spreading evenly. Leave to cool, then cover and chill in the refrigerator until firm.

4 Run a small knife around the edge of each basin. Dip the bases briefly into a bowl of hot water, then turn out the rice onto four serving plates.

5 Scatter the pomegranate seeds over the rice, then sprinkle with grated nutmeg. Serve immediately.

GRILLED FRUIT KEBABS

Serves: 4

Prep: 10 mins
plus marinating

Cook: 10 mins

Ingredients

2 tbsp hazelnut oil

2 tbsp clear honey

juice and finely grated zest of 1 lime

2 pineapple rings, cut into chunks

8 strawberries

1 pear, peeled, cored and thickly sliced

1 banana, peeled and thickly sliced

2 kiwi fruit, peeled and quartered

Method

1 Preheat the grill to medium. Mix the oil, honey and lime juice and zest together in a large, shallow, non-metallic dish. Add the fruit and turn to coat. Cover and leave to marinate for 10 minutes.

2 Thread the fruit alternately onto four long metal skewers, beginning with a piece of pineapple and ending with a strawberry.

3 Brush the kebabs with the marinade and cook under the grill, brushing frequently with the marinade, for 5 minutes. Turn the kebabs over, brush with the remaining marinade and grill for a further 5 minutes. Serve immediately.

BAKING & DESSERTS

OVEN BAKED SOFT-CENTRED CHOCOLATE PUDDING

Serves: 4   **Prep: 15 mins**   **Cook: 20–25 mins**

Ingredients

200 g/7 oz gluten-free dark chocolate, broken into pieces

115 g/4 oz unsalted butter, plus extra for greasing

3 tbsp gluten-free plain flour, sifted

3 eggs, beaten

115 g/4 oz caster sugar

3 tbsp ground almonds

1 tsp gluten-free baking powder

½ tsp vanilla essence

½ tsp glycerine

gluten-free cocoa powder, for dusting

vanilla cream, to serve

Method

1 Preheat the oven to 200°C/400°F/Gas Mark 6.

2 Place the chocolate and butter in a heatproof bowl and set over a pan of simmering water. Stir the mixture until it is just melted and then remove it from the heat.

3 Place the flour, eggs, sugar, almonds, baking powder, vanilla essence and glycerine in a bowl and mix until combined. Slowly stir in the chocolate mixture.

4 Grease four 175 ml/6 fl oz metal dariole moulds. Divide the mixture between the moulds and place on a baking tray. Bake the puddings in the preheated oven for 15–18 minutes.

5 Remove from the oven, gently run a knife around the edge of each pudding and invert onto a serving plate. Dust with cocoa powder and serve immediately with vanilla cream.

MANGO CHEESECAKE

Serves: 8

Prep: 20 mins
plus cooling & chilling

Cook: 40–45 mins

Ingredients

70 g/2½ oz butter, plus extra for greasing

175 g/6 oz gluten-free biscuits, such as digestives, crushed

40 g/1½ oz ground almonds

Filling

1 large mango, stoned, peeled and diced

juice of 1 lemon

200 g/7 oz natural yogurt

1 tbsp gluten-free cornflour

3 tbsp maple syrup

450 g/1 lb cream cheese

Topping

3 tbsp maple syrup

1 small mango, stoned, peeled and sliced

Method

1 Preheat the oven to 180°C/350°F/Gas Mark 4. Lightly grease a 23 cm/9 inch round, loose-bottomed cake tin. To make the biscuit base, melt the butter in a medium-sized saucepan, then stir in the crushed biscuits and almonds. Press the mixture into the base of the prepared cake tin to make an even layer. Bake in the preheated oven for 10 minutes.

2 Meanwhile, to make the filling, put the mango, lemon juice, yogurt, cornflour, maple syrup and cream cheese into a food processor or blender and process until smooth and creamy. Pour the mixture over the biscuit base and smooth with the back of a spoon. Bake for 25–30 minutes, or until golden and set. Leave to cool in the tin, then transfer to a wire rack and chill in the refrigerator for 30 minutes to firm up.

3 To make the topping, heat the maple syrup in a frying pan. Brush the top of the cheesecake with the maple syrup. Add the mango to the remaining maple syrup in the pan and cook for 1 minute, stirring. Leave to cool slightly, then arrange the mango slices on top of the cheesecake. Pour over any remaining syrup before serving.

COCONUT MILK & STRAWBERRY ICE CREAM

Serves: 6

Prep: 30 mins
plus freezing

Cook: none

Ingredients

450 g/1 lb strawberries, hulled and halved

400 ml/14 fl oz canned full-fat coconut milk

85 g/3 oz clear honey

Method

1 Purée the strawberries in a food processor or liquidizer, then press through a sieve set over a mixing bowl to remove the seeds.

2 Add the coconut milk and honey to the strawberry purée and whisk together.

3 Pour the mixture into a large roasting tin to a depth of 2 cm/¾ inch, cover the top of the tin with clingfilm, then freeze for about 2 hours until just set.

4 Scoop back into the food processor or liquidizer and blitz again until smooth to break down the ice crystals. Pour into a plastic container or 900-g/2-lb loaf tin lined with non-stick baking paper. Place the lid on the plastic container or fold the paper over the ice cream in the loaf tin. Return to the freezer for 3–4 hours, or until firm enough to scoop.

5 Serve immediately or leave in the freezer overnight or until needed. Thaw at room temperature for 15 minutes to soften slightly, then scoop into individual dishes to serve.

INDEX

INDEX

This edition published by Parragon Books Ltd in 2016
LOVE FOOD is an imprint of Parragon Books Ltd

Parragon Books Ltd
Chartist House
15–17 Trim Street
Bath BA1 1HA, UK
www.parragon.com/lovefood

ISBN 978-1-4748-3794-1

Printed in China

Introduction by Anne Sheasby
New recipes by Georgina Fuggle
Cover photography and new photography by Al Richardson
The cover shows the Courgette Quiche on page 132.

Notes for the Reader
This book uses both metric and imperial measurements. Follow the same units of measurement throughout; do not mix metric and imperial. All spoon measurements are level: teaspoons are assumed to be 5 ml, and tablespoons are assumed to be 15 ml. Unless otherwise stated, milk is assumed to be full fat, eggs and individual fruits and vegetables are medium, pepper is freshly ground black pepper and salt is table salt. A pinch of salt is calculated as 1/16 of a teaspoon. Unless otherwise stated, all root vegetables should be peeled prior to using.

The times given are an approximate guide only. Preparation times differ according to the techniques used by different people and the cooking times may also vary from those given.

While the publisher of the book and the original author(s) of the recipes and other text have made all reasonable efforts to ensure that the information contained in this book is accurate and up to date at the time of publication, anyone reading this book should note the following important points: -

* Medical and pharmaceutical knowledge is constantly changing and the author(s) and the publisher cannot and do not guarantee the accuracy or appropriateness of the contents of this book;
* In any event, this book is not intended to be, and should not be relied upon as a substitute for appropriate, tailored professional advice. The author(s) and the publisher strongly recommend that a doctor or other healthcare professional is consulted before embarking on major dietary changes;
* For the reasons set out above, and to the fullest extent permitted by law, the author(s) and publisher: (i) cannot and do not accept any legal duty of care or responsibility in relation to the accuracy or appropriateness of the contents of this book, even where expressed as 'advice' or using other words to this effect; and (ii) disclaim any liability, loss, damage or risk that may be claimed or incurred as a consequence – directly or indirectly – of the use and/or application of any of the contents of this book.

The publisher has been careful to select recipes that contain gluten-free products. Any ready-made ingredients that could potentially contain gluten have been listed as gluten free, so readers know to check they are gluten free. However, always read labels carefully and, if necessary, check with the manufacturer.

SOUR CHERRY & CINNAMON SCONES

Makes: 8   **Prep: 15 mins**   **Cook: 20 mins**

Ingredients

250 g/9 oz gluten-free self-raising flour

1 tsp gluten-free baking powder

50 g/1¾ oz unsalted butter

50 g/1¾ oz caster sugar

50 g/1¾ oz dried cherries, chopped

½ tsp ground cinnamon

1 egg

1 egg, beaten, to glaze

150 ml/5 fl oz milk

1–2 tbsp demerara sugar, for sprinkling

Method

1 Preheat the oven to 200°C/400°F/Gas Mark 6.

2 Sift the flour and baking powder into a bowl. Using your fingertips, rub the butter into the flour mixture until it resembles fine breadcrumbs. Stir through the sugar, chopped cherries and the cinnamon.

3 Lightly beat together the egg and milk in a separate bowl. Add this to the flour mixture and beat to give a smooth consistency.

4 Scoop 7–9 mounds of the scone mixture onto a lined baking tray using a deep spoon or an ice cream scoop. Brush some of the beaten egg over the top of each scone and sprinkle over the demerara sugar.

5 Bake the scones in the centre of the oven for 15–18 minutes, or until they are a light golden colour. Remove the baking tray from the oven and slide the scones onto a wire rack to cool. Serve the scones while they are warm.